# NO SUCH THING AS A
# FREE RIDE?

## A COLLECTION OF HITCHERS' TALES

# NO SUCH THING AS A

# FREE

# RIDE?

## A COLLECTION OF HITCHERS' TALES

Compiled and edited
by Simon Sykes and Tom Sykes

This book is dedicated to Peggy Barrett (1921-2004)
and to Patricia Pearse (1927-1969).

Inspirational in all ways.

First published in Great Britain in 2005 by Cassell Illustrated,
a division of Octopus Publishing Group Limited
2-4 Heron Quays, London E14 4JP

Compiled and edited by Simon Sykes and Tom Sykes
Designed by John Round Design

A CIP catalogue record for this book is available from the British
Library.

ISBN  1 84403 382 1
EAN 9781844033829

Printed in Spain


Picture credits
Front cover: Getty Images
All other images: Alamy Images


Acknowledgements
Our gratitude goes to all our contributors and our family and
friends who encouraged and supported our efforts to bring this
book to publication. Also particular thanks to Gabrielle Mander
and the team at Cassell for their hard work and patience.

# CONTENTS

# INTRODUCTION

Mention hitch-hiking in any gathering and someone always has a story to tell or a view to express. Some, with the passing of time, might seem the most unlikely candidates to recount how they set off one day to travel wherever they chose, oblivious to lack of funds or detailed itinerary, motivated by curiosity and the promise of adventure. Some will have stories of hitching out of necessity – stuck somewhere and the solution apparent by simply sticking out their thumb, knowing full well that someone would eventually stop and give them a lift. Others might never have hitched and yet still tell stories second- or third-hand. The nature of the tales sometimes provokes further debate, since the fundamental idea of begging a lift from strangers on the open road seems on the face of it an unlikely and somewhat risky – even irresponsible – undertaking; the same applies to anyone responding to the hitcher. But one person's risk is another's adventure – paranoia or derring-do, or faith in human nature?

Some contend that is was all simpler 'back then', in some unspecified time when hitching was the chosen method of transport amongst mostly young people in the West. They would say you started out naïve and came back worldly; a fully cynical humanist, knowledgeable about the strengths and weaknesses of the human race. You became a wiser person having undertaken a particularly intense rite of passage. Where else could you converse politely with kind old ladies, listen to the woes of a travelling salesman, feign admiration for a sad character masquerading as a special forces operative, make a friend for life, obtain gainful employment, laugh until your sides ache, make swift judgements about human beings that determine your destination in every sense! – and all in one day in a country far away?

That hitch-hiking's heyday had apparently gone forever unrecorded for posterity seemed a pity.

So in 1999 we started collecting stories for this book, mindful that the contributions would be interesting and varied and sometimes unashamedly nostalgic. What we hadn't bargained for was evidence of hitching's continuing popularity and relevance around the world. We discovered that the legacy of that halcyon age had inspired various networks, clubs, communities, websites, and even an International Hitch-Hiking Conference held annually in Vilnius. Hitching seems most popular in places where poverty and shortage reign, or where public transport is deficient. Here there is a sense of mutual assistance which has largely disappeared from the affluent areas of the world. Moreover, hitch-hiking might just have a more profound role to play, as part of wider transport initiatives to conserve our resources and protect our environment.

At the time of writing, there is talk amongst British politicians of all stripes about earmarking motorway lanes for car sharers. For years the Cuban government has sponsored over 1,000 official 'car-stops' in Havana alone. State inspectors halt oncoming motorists and hook them up with hitchers heading the same way. In this book, alongside the great stories, you will find practical proposals for regulated, effective hitch-hiking aimed at enabling people to travel responsibly in every sense.

As the book developed, we became curious about the history of hitching. Although there is little serious scholarship on the subject, the scant evidence would suggest that it is as old as transport itself. In North America in the 19th and early 20th centuries, a common (if illegal) practice was to 'ride the rails' by boarding passing trains without paying the fare. By the 1920s, with the expansion of automobile ownership around the developed world, the practice of motorists giving lifts to complete strangers had become well-established. During the Depression in the US, hitch-hiking benefited from another boom in popularity, so much so that the federal government established over 300 Transient Bureau Centres in the mid-1930s to assist (usually poor, homeless) hitchers. It was clear that poverty and limited public transportation was the *raison d'être* for the early hitch-hikers.

This book deals largely with the period post-1950 when hitch-hiking came to be associated with a broader youth culture. The Romantic motif of The Road as a means to adventure, risk-taking and mind expansion is well-represented in the arts, from novels like *On the Road* and *Fear and Loathing in Las Vegas*, to films like *Easy Rider* and *The Motorcycle Diaries*, and music by artists such as Woody Guthrie, Bob Dylan, The Grateful Dead, Marvin Gaye and The Sugarcubes. However hitch-hiking itself is woefully under-reported or simply slandered: consider those countless films featuring a pleasant, law-abiding couple who pick up a psychotic loon hell-bent on doing something unspeakably nasty to them. In the West from the 1980s, a few hyped incidents of murder and robbery created a regrettable climate of fear around hitch-hiking. Of course there is an element of risk, but there is an element of risk in every method of transport.

In the last twenty years in the USA and Western Europe, the cult of the selfish individual has created a sense that every person is an island, their home a castle with drawbridge raised, their car a steel bubble not to be intruded upon. People are suspicious of their neighbours just as they are suspicious of strangers on the roadside. A sad atomisation of our communities has taken place over the years, leading to a breakdown in trust and communication. Hitching by its nature implies a cooperative spirit – a bit more of which we might all benefit from.

It was always our intention to make the book a page-turner, crammed full of gripping yarns, comic anecdotes, outrageous recollections, lively polemic as well as a deeper tribute to the cultural and social significance of hitch-hiking, worldwide, past and present.

We decided to section the book into vaguely themed chapters to lend some order to an impressive volume of contributions. The titles are largely self-explanatory and there is an inevitable crossover between chapters. 'Views of the Highway' comprises essays and observations about hitching; 'Good Trips' and 'Bad Trips' are simply that, although some good things happen in 'Bad Trips' and vice versa; 'A Lift Less Ordinary' is devoted to the stranger journeys; 'Patrons and Passengers' explores the relationship between those who hitch and those who pick up; 'Epochal Intersections' illustrates how a simple lift can sometimes land you in the presence of famous people and history in the making; 'Let's Improvise' concerns those hitchers who have to think creatively and unconventionally; and 'Snapshots of a Destination' contains stories which convey a strong sense of place. We have also added a section of further reading, music and films which make reference to hitching, as well as links to information on the web. This is by no means an exhaustive list, more a sample of what may be out there…

We have been so encouraged by the level of interest and the quality of the writing that we are already planning a sequel. We'd love to receive any views, stories, essays or feedback from any readers. Please contact us on **hitchtales@hotmail.com** or on our website: **www.hitchtales.com**

SIMON SYKES AND TOM SYKES

# Views of
# the Highway

# Max Hastings <small>author and journalist</small>

Every Friday afternoon in term time, and a good many other days too, at the roundabout on the London road out of Oxford, a queue of undergraduates might be glimpsed, thumbs extended and hope in their hearts. There was seldom long to wait in those days, forty-odd years ago. Hitching was so much part of the culture of the times that giving and taking lifts was commonplace. Bored commercial travellers, lonely truck drivers, even an occasional housewife, would give any plausible-looking hitcher a lift.

I was sometimes amazed by the poor technique of the suppliants: glowering faces, shambolic appearance. Me, I often hitched in a jacket and tie, and always with a beaming, imbecilic grin. I travelled that way from one end of Britain to the other, and across Europe to Istanbul as well, though catching lifts in Italy was much harder than in England. During my brief dalliance with the military, I would always hitch in battledress and red beret, because in the sixties almost every man in Britain had done national service, and would give a soldier a ride from nostalgia or fellow-feeling. Hitching was not merely a means of getting about; it was a culture, and one that I loved. One met a huge range of people, had a lot of great conversations, and often met kindness and generosity. Today, when fear of rapists and paedophiles, muggers and mass murderers seems to have taken over Britain, I fancy that if I stood on the roundabout at Oxford in a white tie and tails, I would have a very long wait for a ride to anywhere. Students are now much better off, travel by public transport is relatively cheaper, and in the age of litigation and the compensation culture, truckers are forbidden on pain of dire penalties to pick up any unauthorised passenger.

I tell my children what they have missed, and they do not believe me for a minute. Yet hitch-hiking exposed a middle-class adolescent to a range of encounters and experiences that were tremendously rewarding, if one came from as sheltered a life as I did. Unkind people said that it was just a form of scrounging, sponging. Not so, I think. The people who gave the rides gained as much from doing so as those of us who accepted them. Hitching was a hangover from the wartime era, really, a time when the nation was all in it together, when the only way people could get through was by sharing and mucking in. For years after I acquired a car, I gave hitchers lifts whenever I could, in gratitude for my own rides. Year by year, however, one saw their numbers diminish. Those who persisted seemed scruffier, more sullen, less inviting. Or maybe I got older and more remote from my own experience. Anyway, I cherish the memory of the three or four hitching years of my life – and the debt to the people who carried me across England and Europe.

# George Monbiot journalist

### 'The Severed Thumb'

When I get sent to Hell, I won't be plunged into the fiery furnace. The Devil will turn me, instead, into a professional driver. I will be damned to spend eternity driving around that first circle of torment, the M25, stressed-out, furious and, above all, isolated from my fellow human beings. I will be deprived of the only possible benefit of car journeys: talking to someone with that strange intensity which sometimes accompanies a conversation held at speed. My fate, in other words, will be that of the millions of lost souls whom our diabolically stupid transport policies condemn to travel alone.

There used to be salvation on the trunk road network. Just a few years ago, on almost every motorway junction stood a man or woman with a rucksack and a piece of cardboard. The company, it has to be said, was of variable quality, but it was company none the less. Today, on the rare occasions on which I borrow one of the devil's chariots, I find the curbs empty. The tourists and poorer residents taking advantage of private transport's preposterous over-capacity have been driven off the roads.

It's not entirely surprising that the hitch-hikers have disappeared. The unpredictability of those encounters contained, of course, a hazard, for both drivers and hikers. The terrible death of the French tourist Celine Figard, three years ago, effectively brought hitch-hiking in Britain to an end. Even before she was killed, the practice had attracted so much unfair publicity and so many spooky films that everyone standing on the verge had begun to look like either a psychopath or a victim.

But something else has happened which has kept the poor and footloose off the roads. Offering people lifts was one of the last outlets for hospitality in a land in which almost all other forms have disappeared. Mrs Thatcher's announcement that there was no such thing as society was not a belief but a manifesto. Her programme was achieved with remarkable speed.

Shared households were broken up. Houseboats, gypsies and travellers were purged. Public transport was run down and people forced into cars, in which the most articulate communication is the shaken fist. And everything, visible or otherwise, was given a cost. No one would do anything for anyone unless there was an immediate material advantage for themselves. Indeed, human interaction became an official liability: lorry drivers picking up hitch-hikers can be dismissed for 'invalidating their insurance.'

Today, almost the only people still hitch-hiking are the people employed to deliver cars. And, in this case, our residual hospitality is being ruthlessly exploited. The delivery people are paid just £50 a day, from which they must find their own expenses. If they took the train back home, in other words, they would wipe out all their earnings. Forcing them to hitch is the perfect externalisation of their employers' costs: by helping the individuals, we're subsidising one of the most vicious business practices in Britain. But it might just be possible to rescue one of the last means we possess to meet strangers in Britain. The social justice campaigner Guy Horton has devised a scheme which could cross both the barrier of fear and the barrier of selfishness. He proposes a sort of hitch-hikers' guild. Members, who would pay a small fee, could be screened: anyone with a record of violent crime would be excluded. The guild would set a rate per mile at which the hiker could contribute to the motorists' costs. It would be much cheaper than most public transport, but just enough to encourage drivers to pick people up.

Drivers would get a windscreen sticker, hitch-hikers a placard, to show that they had joined the club. A more sophisticated system, arranged on the Net, might allow drivers and hikers to organise a pickup point. If members had to submit a password, this would also leave a record of who had picked up whom.

It might all sound a little far-fetched, but an informal, unvetted scheme a bit like this runs in Poland: hitch-hikers buy coupons which can be exchanged for petrol by the motorists who pick them up. Hitching, as a result, remains an important mode of transport. Cars are generally full, so the roads are less congested, the poor can travel almost as easily as the rich and, astonishingly, people even talk to each other. It could just be the means by which a spot of the social glue that Mrs Thatcher dissolved is allowed to set once more.

## Steven Pinker Johnstone Family Professor of Psychology at Harvard University

I don't think anyone will have experiences like this again. They depend on real or virtual communities to which drivers and hitch-hikers feel they both belong. Those communities seem to have dissolved. Today the fear of foul play prevents everyone but daredevils from inviting a stranger into their car or entering the car of a stranger.

## Stephen Regan Professor of English at the University of Durham and author of books and essays on modern poetry

### 'Hitching a Ride'

Looking back, it seems as if the 1970s was a decade of glorious summers. It must have rained sometimes, though my recollections of standing at the roadside and hitching lifts all over England are blessed with sunshine. Hitching a ride was nearly always an opportunity for youthful adventure and never just an admission of being broke. Of course, we were always hard up, having just bought a new guitar or a couple of double albums by our favourite bands, but it was the romance of the road that drew us to the same grassy verges year after year on epic journeys south. With a few T-shirts, a spare pair of Levi's and a bag of sandwiches, we would sail off on some magical odyssey, pulled by instinct as surely as the swallows twittering overhead. It was just the natural and obvious way to go.

John D. was my travelling companion. His blond hair and faded blue denim made him a prince of the road. He would pick up his guitar and play some childhood tune like 'Tales From the Riverbank' with intense concentration. We would spend hours singing our favourite songs, so that memories of hitching a ride would be forever musical. We probably imagined that in some modest way we were doing what Woody Guthrie and Bob Dylan had done on vast American highways. So many of the songs we knew were songs about hitting the road and leaving the discontents of life behind. In our case, we were probably giving a big wave to the Sisters of Mercy who ruled our hearts and minds in a convent school in County Durham. Hitching a ride was a kind of truancy, a shaking free from convention.

For a long time our favourite album was Cat Stevens' *Tea For the Tillerman*. John D. had a striking likeness to Cat's session guitarist, Alun Davies, and he could have stepped in any time to play guitar on 'Father and Son' or 'Where Do the Children Play?' *Tea For the Tillerman* seemed made for the road and we suspected that Cat had probably composed most of the songs just north of Hendon where you can easily get access to the M1. It was hardly surprising that Ian Dury formed a band called 'Kilburn and the High Roads' around that time. We would while away the hours in between lifts with perfectly felicitous lyrics: 'Well, I left my happy home to see what I could find out. I left my folk and friends with the aim to clear my mind out'. Those lines are from the aptly titled 'On the Road to Find Out', but the most fitting song of all was 'Miles From Nowhere'. How did it go? 'Miles from nowhere, guess I'll take my time, oh yeah, to reach there'. At one point, you have to scream 'Miles from Nowhere' if you really want to emulate Cat Stevens, and since the slip roads of the M1 are usually pretty empty it was never a problem if you wanted to scream your heart out on the way back to Durham.

Hitching a ride had its own strange choreography. Every act of hopeful waiting was a studied rehearsal for the drama of the ride itself. Samuel Beckett must have written *Waiting for Godot* with two stranded hitch-hikers in mind. Always, of course, the performance involved a ritualistic leaning out to the road with arm fully stretched and thumb straight up. Frequently, as the day wore on and cars drove by, the hopeful thumb would repeatedly turn into two fingers and the anxious silence would be broken with derisory cries of 'Bastard!' Sometimes a car would pull over unexpectedly just as these insults were being launched and we would walk towards it slowly and get in cautiously, not knowing if our greetings had caused a sudden change of heart or if the driver was blithely unaware of the bucket of filth we had just emptied on his head.

John D. and I were still in our early teens when we started hitching long-distance rides. We spent a couple of summers fruit-picking at a place called Friday Bridge in rural Cambridgeshire and we learned the ways of the road on complicated journeys home. We had just enough sense of geography to know that we should aim for Peterborough and try to get on the A1. We would start out bright and early and get a lift immediately with a local tradesman, only to find that he was going no further than five or six miles up the road. After a series of these local lifts, we would eventually reach a main road and hope that the next lift would take us to the motorway. We had incredible good luck on the A1, sometimes getting home in just a few hours, perched on planks of wood in the back of a joiner's van or riding high in the cab of an articulated truck.

There were disappointments and humiliations as well. To stand on the roadside for hours on end is to flirt with chance and to face the possibility that you might still be there the following morning. Occasionally, you would get a lift that took you where you didn't want to go and made your journey considerably longer. John D. and I once ended up in Leicester city centre when a fussy P.E. teacher concerned for our welfare removed us from the motorway and advised us to take the train back home. After wasting hours trying to thumb a lift out of the city centre on a busy Saturday afternoon, we paid for a taxi to take us back to where we had started out and eventually caught another lift in the right direction.

Even worse, we had to beg a lift from a lorry driver at a café in Wetherby late one night after he had twice told us in no uncertain terms that he had no interest in hitch-hikers. We usually kept quiet about these embarrassing failures, but they were all part of a rich learning experience that would be handed down to younger lads in times ahead. To quote that lovely song that Crosby, Stills, Nash and Young used to sing: 'You who are on the road must have a code that you can live by'. It was a code very different from the usual Highway Code.

Part of that code was knowing how to converse with the driver of the vehicle you had just flagged down at the edge of the motorway. Most drivers were happy to have some company and would amiably chat away for hours until you saw your hometown in the distance. Some of them were hard work and you had to be careful not to exceed the limits of hitch-hiking garrulousness. John D. was always happy to let me do the bulk of the talking. My Irish ancestry ensured that I had just the right amount of blarney to keep the driver mildly amused for a couple of hundred miles. It was good practice for what I would later come to know in academic circles as 'discourse theory'. I would usually open with the inevitable bluster, "How far are you going, mate?" and having ensured that it was worth the ride, I would follow up with the equally predictable question, "So do you do this trip very often?" These were cringe-making salutations, a bit like asking a girl you fancied what she did in her spare time, but they were necessary and expected parts of the discourse.

Once you settled into a nice seventy miles per hour, you could broaden the horizons and embrace any variety of idle, useless chatter, depending on the humour and intellect of the driver. On an average journey you could easily cover pets, family, holidays (or even family holidays), religion, television, football and the state of the nation. If there was a lull in the conversation, I would gladly fill it by talking about the mysteries of pigeon racing, something I could rattle on about with unflagging enthusiasm and insight. John D. and I would sometimes rehearse these pointless conversations for the benefit of friends down at the pub. One of us would pretend to be the driver, lifting a pint of Guinness up and down as if gripping the steering wheel, while the other tried out various banal expressions and enquiries: "So what do you do for a living, mate?" or "How long have you had this car?" Conducting these exchanges up and down the M1 and the A1 did have a special value in acquainting us at a very early stage with the English mind in all its glorious pomposity and stupidity. We became remarkably adept at distinguishing dyed-in-the-wool Tories from Labour sympathisers, and we took great delight in letting the upholders of the establishment vent their rage against working-class agitators while we gleefully provoked them into ever more extreme and rancorous denunciations of their fellow citizens.

As in the world at large, politics and religion could be tricky subjects to engage with in the microcosm of a Ford Granada or a Morris Minor. I remember my tutor, Professor John Unrau, telling me how he first confronted the contradictions of the British class system when he came from Canada to Oxford as a Rhodes Scholar. He was hitching a lift from Oxford to Liverpool on the way to see his Irish girlfriend in Dublin. He was offered a lift with a lorry driver who was keen to hear about student life at Oxford University. John, being a political radical and a disciple of John Ruskin, took great pleasure in denouncing the inequalities of the British education system and the detestable snobbishness of Oxford. Thinking that this would undoubtedly be pleasant music to the ears of the lorry driver, he went on to castigate the appalling standards of tuition at Oxford and the pathetic narcissism of his tutors. To his astonishment, the lorry driver burned with incandescent rage and threatened to throw him out of the cab for daring as an upstart colonial to question the greatness of Oxford. John suddenly remembered that he had to visit a relative in the West Midlands and asked if he could be let off long before they reached Liverpool.

Drivers had a variety of reasons for stopping and offering lifts to hitch-hikers, and not all of them were inspired by simple human kindness. Sometimes there would be a surreptitious motive that would gradually emerge a few miles down the road. One afternoon, I was overjoyed to be offered a lift home in a shining new Mercedes saloon. The only shortcoming was that the driver of the car was completely exhausted and had only stopped because he needed someone to talk to him incessantly and occasionally prod him out of sleep. After a few miles, we swapped places and I drove the new Mercedes over two hundred miles north while the grateful, trusting owner slept soundly in the passenger seat.

On another occasion, I was asked by a recent graduate of the University of Warwick if I would roll illegal cigarettes for him while he blissfully careered along in a delivery van trailing clouds of marijuana smoke. When I asked him where he was going, he looked confounded and gave me the memorable hip reply: "I don't know man, I just drive on the road."

I was once travelling back from Windsor Free Festival with a friend called Phil Carson, whose nickname was Cass. We stopped a car after only ten minutes and were amazed when the driver told us he would take us anywhere we wanted to go. This euphoria began to evaporate when we got a closer look at him. From the back seat we could see his shifty eyes darting about in his mirror and we noticed he was unshaven and even more unkempt than we were after sleeping in a muddy field for three days. He had very few teeth and seemed to splutter his words in a thoroughly lascivious and disagreeable manner. More worrying still, he turned off the main road after only fifteen or twenty minutes and began to drive through a series of small villages somewhere in Berkshire. When we quizzed him about this, he mumbled something about wanting to show us where he lived. Cass and I looked at each other, knowing that we were in the company of some wretched pervert, but not having much sense of what to do. We were probably both imagining that we had just got caught up in some awful sub-Hitchcock movie and the only solutions we could envisage were the ones we had seen in the cinema, where invariably the captive teenagers were strangled with electrical flex and later dissected. I tried the palliative approach, calmly explaining that we didn't have time for tea at the vicarage and that Durham was a long way north. The driver just stared ahead, oblivious to all reasoning. I could see that Cass was on edge and quickly losing patience. He suddenly leaned forward and shouted, "If you don't take us back to the motorway right now, we are going to bray your fucking head in." That seemed to do the trick. The driver turned back, delivered us to the motorway, and politely said goodbye. It was a strange warning of how things could sometimes go badly wrong in these chance encounters on the road.

Maybe that anxious drive to an uncertain destination is one explanation for the scarcity of hitch-hikers on the road today. The risks have been made all too apparent with the massive publicity given to a few high profile cases where young people have gone missing. The suspect is known only by a white van or a red sports car. I still see men carrying number plates, having delivered a new car to some distant place, then trying their luck with a courtesy lift and saving the rail fare home. I never see the ghostly revenants of myself and John D. The few hitch-hikers on British roads tend to come from Spain or Italy or Australia. They seem oddly out of place in this changed environment where more and more young people have their own cars and would think it an act of utter lunacy to stand for hours at the edge of a motorway with their thumbs in the wind. I would be hard pushed to explain to them the thrill of setting out for a long journey without a bus ticket or a rail pass. Just now and again, I remember the joy of a car stopping on a bright morning and the laughable recourse to the time-honoured formula: "Are you going far, mate?"

Now I'm about to take the road north again. I'm going back home to start a new job as Professor of English at the University of Durham. I ought to hitch a ride, but I have too many books and other bits of lumber to carry with me. My reference point these days is Philip Larkin's salutary reflection on 'clearing off' in 'Poetry of Departures'. The speaker of that poem imagines what it might be like to 'swagger the nut-strewn roads', only to reconcile himself to 'Books; china; a life/Reprehensibly perfect'. Life is still that long road ahead. It's just that these days it seems to get dark sooner and there are fewer lifts to help you along the way. Miles from nowhere, guess I'll take my time, oh yeah, to reach there.

# Gabriel Morris for more information on the author, visit his website at gabrielmorris.bravehost.com

### 'Transportation Recycling – A Hitch-hiker's Perspective to Thumbing Around'

A couple of summers ago, I was stuck hitching across Wisconsin, trying to make it to Minneapolis to catch a flight back home to Portland, Oregon later that evening. My prospects of actually buckling into a seat on that plane were looking more and more grim. I was on my way back from a festival in Michigan's Upper Peninsula and had given myself two days—two days—to cover a seven-hour drive. After covering a pathetic fifty miles the first day, I'd spent the night on the lawn of a rest stop, then crawled out of my sleeping bag at 4:30 am and unravelled my thumb at first light.

The problem was, nobody was going to Minneapolis. They were all headed for a cool lake somewhere—judging by the boats dragging behind every vehicle—and bringing a stranger along for the ride was the furthest thing from their minds. Besides, it appeared they hadn't seen a hippie around here since '69. There wasn't a welcoming vibe emanating from behind their windshields. By one o'clock that afternoon, I'd made it another fifty miles. That's seven miles an hour. I still had a five-hour drive ahead of me, and only eight hours before the plane departed the tarmac. Given my progress so far, it would be days before I saw Minnesota. It was starting to look like one hell of a goddamn hitch back to Oregon.

Hitch-hikers sure have it rough these days. I speak from many road-weary days of experience. In our modern-day, mechanized society, obsessed with prosperity, self-reliance and automobile worship, if you don't have your own vehicle by the age of eighteen or so, then you're not getting with the program. And if you should have the gall to stand on the side of the road with a backpack and a protruding thumb, expecting someone else to carry you to your destination free of charge, then you're simply derelict. As a hitch-hiker today, you don't even get the consideration of being a free-spirited, soul-searching counter-culturalist. It ain't the sixties anymore. Stand on the side of any American roadway and you'll soon get the point. You're just in the wrong place, at the wrong time. Take a hike and get a job.

Having hitch-hiked on and off for more than twenty years (I started as a kid to shorten the walk home after school) in fifteen states and seven countries, I resent this substandard status. I'm not a bum, I'm not a freeloader, I'm not a criminal—I'm just adventurous. I hitch-hike because it's a thrill, because it's convenient, because I get acquainted with all types of interesting characters, and sure, because it's damn cheap. So what's wrong with asking a fellow citizen to take you where they're already going, in exchange for a little company and some good karma?

From a practical standpoint, it seems the stigma around hitch-hiking is a reflection of a dysfunctional society. In a culture where people actually trusted one another—if you can imagine that—there would be few good reasons why a person with an empty seat should pass another person in need of a ride. Giving someone a lift when headed in the same direction should be no less socially expected than, say, donating one's used items to thrift stores to be utilized by someone else. It's just a reasonable, efficient use of energy and resources. Hitch-hiking is the transportation equivalent of recycling. And it seems anything that lessens the strain on our overburdened planet is worth taking the time to look into. Hitch-hiking may sound like an extreme method to many for getting from one place to another—but it all depends on your perspective.

I remember my father telling stories of picking up hitch-hikers when he was younger. This was in the early seventies, around the time I was born. My parents lived near Vancouver, Canada for a few years and almost every morning on his way into town to work, my dad would pick up a few folks… and then again on his way home each evening. It was just normal, even expected—especially when, as in my dad's case, you had a beard and longish hair. You weren't just picking up a stranger, but a fellow seeker of truth and explorer of life. If you didn't know anything about one another yet, then you would, not far down the road. And you'd probably be a more open-minded and compassionate person for it.

Maybe it's just fabricated nostalgia on my part, but those sound like the glory days for hitch-hikers and assorted wanderers, at least in modern history. A shame that I was in diapers. Of course, there are remnants of that bygone era left—or I wouldn't have my own gypsy tales to share, hitch-hiking the length of the United Kingdom and parts of Europe, and criss-crossing the West. You can still stick your neck, and your thumb, out there. It's perfectly legal to hitch-hike in most of the U.S.—and crazy, in my opinion, that it's technically against the law in a few states, including Montana, Utah, Nevada, Wyoming and Wisconsin. Even in those states, however, all of which I've hitched successfully, you can generally get away with it if you keep a low profile and stay out of trouble.

It always helps things to go smoothly, of course, if you can present yourself as someone who seems generally friendly and harmless. Choose a place to stand where there's plenty of room for cars to pull over, so that a cop won't pull up instead, tell you they're concerned for your safety, then run your ID and possibly hand you a ticket. Also, hitch-hiking on interstates and freeways is illegal—but you can still hitch-hike on the on-ramp. Just lean your pack up against the sign that says 'pedestrians prohibited.' There's usually a good pullout right there anyway, and cars haven't yet picked up much speed. If they're flying along at sixty-five on the freeway, they'll be less inclined to pull over than if they're just getting into gear.

If you're headed for a specific destination, making a sign can be helpful. Don't waste your time, however, if all you have is a piece of paper and a ballpoint pen. They'll never get the chance to read it. Instead, use a hefty piece of cardboard and a big, black marker, with as little to decipher as possible. i.e., if you're headed for San Francisco, California, just put 'CA' or 'CALI' if you're not yet in the state or else 'S.F.' if you're getting close enough that people will know where you're referring to. Don't try to explain your entire predicament in the hopes of attracting sympathy, i.e. "Just got kicked out of the army, homeless, unemployed, no girlfriend, and I really need a ride to my grandma's for a shoulder to cry on." That might work if you can catch people hanging out at a stoplight, with a few minutes on their hands. But in my experience, getting a ride from the centre of town is near impossible. Take the time to catch a bus or hike out to the edge of the city, where the people going by are more likely to be covering some distance.

With all this in mind, try to put a pleasant expression on your face, don't take the occasional middle-finger or thumbs-down too personally, and be willing to wait. Sometimes, you get a ride before you even get your thumb out there; others, it could take a couple of hours. My longest wait, in Alaska, was about ten hours. That can make you seriously stir-crazy. A hacky-sack, journal or good book can come in handy for passing the time. But if you can hang in there, chances are that eventually someone will pull through for you. Only twice in twenty years did I ever get so fed up that I hopped a bus. If you just keep putting a positive vibe out there, someone with a heart and a little nerve (and probably some similar experience) will likely reciprocate by taking you a little further down the road. Of course, keeping up that positivity can be a challenge at times—especially if you have a plane to catch. The looks you get from most people now while waiting for that sought-after ride are often downright dismal. It seems the only plausible reason for hitch-hiking in many people's eyes is that you were just booted from the local penitentiary.

Everybody has heard a hitch-hiking horror story or two. Unfortunately, these are the only images that make it anywhere near the societal subconscious. I've hitch-hiked sporadically since I was about eight, and extensively throughout my twenties, and have honestly never had a bad experience. Questionable characters? Sure. Freaks? Plenty. But I've never felt endangered. On the other hand, I was once mugged while walking down the street. This doesn't keep me from continuing to walk down the street. If you think about it, is it any riskier these days to get into a stranger's car or give one a ride, than it is to hop on a Greyhound bus with forty or fifty strangers, all of whom are about as broke as you, many of them less emotionally stable? I've seen in the news lately plenty of violent and bizarre confrontations occurring on public buses. But none involving hitch-hiking incidents. This doesn't mean that shit doesn't happen. But shit can happen anywhere.

And yet, I can certainly understand people's concerns when it comes to picking up strangers, especially the shadowy-looking folks who tend to hang out on the side of the road. Even I don't pick up a lot of hitchers when driving. Either I'm just grooving along in my own space, enjoying the solo ride or else I can't trust the look of the character, and you never know. Hitch-hiking could be compared to surfing. The chances of actually getting attacked by a shark are extremely minimal to none. You have better odds of winning millions in the lottery. Still, if you look down into the ocean and let your fears take over, it can be enough to keep you out of the water. But the thing is, the more people in the water—or out on the road—the less chance of getting bitten.

Speaking of which, back to the glory days of less fear and more love, when multitudes of wanderers felt that impulse to let their hair down and open their hearts, take a chance and explore the country, their thumbs guiding the way. It seems that it's a positive development in a society's evolution when strangers feel more inclined to rely on one another, and to help each other out. Isn't this, to some extent, the whole point of our human coexistence? A healthy society should be an interdependent one. It seems a damn shame that we live in a world where you so often can't trust your fellow citizens. One can only hope that this trend has the chance to turn around, and those free-roaming days can return in some form, along with a little more peace, love and goodwill. Hitch-hikers deserve some more respect. Hey, if nothing else, at least it's one less car.

And, in case you were wondering, I did manage to catch that plane out of Minneapolis. At about 1:30 in the afternoon, a minivan flew by me. I gave a half-wave of understanding at the blur of passengers as they sailed by. A half-mile down the road, however, the vehicle screeched to a halt, turned around, came back, and pulled up in front of me. The male driver rolled down the window.

"Where ya headed?" he asked.

"Minneapolis!" I tried to say with enough exuberance to win him over, in case he was scoping me out.

"Same here. Jump on in."

A minute later, my whole attitude towards life had shifted. I was flying down the road at no charge, chatting with a local family, sipping on a root beer they handed me cold from the cooler. Although we'd never met before, and would probably never see one another again, there was plenty of conversational ground to cover. This was what hitch-hiking was all about. I was, of course, infinitely grateful for the ride. And they were glad they could help someone out, obviously stuck in a rough spot. He said that he'd decided to pick me up because of that half-wave of mine. Anyone who could still manage a little friendliness after getting passed by deserved a helping hand. I guess, in this case, some good karma came back to me. I made it to the airport with time to spare; and soon enough was buckling myself into that seat with a certain pride that, once again, my thumb had managed to pull me through.

# Richard Stokoe political advisor

At Lancaster University there is an alternative to public transport in the form of the 'hitching post.' Basically the university is four miles from the city centre, just along South Road in Lancaster. Outside number 10 is a lamppost where you can stick your thumb out and people will know that you are travelling to the Uni. Rather than paying the 50p to get up to the Uni, hundreds of lifts would be given and received. This also applied for getting back into town, where there was even a shelter. (Just looking at the website it appears that it has been refurbished!) You could get everything from Rolls-Royces, to 2CVs to HGVs stopping by – no end of entertainment – and as far as I am aware it has never been abused yet!

# Gareth Rees writer, artist, musician

I'd seen icebergs and whales spouting. I saw royal palms in Florida and lemons and grapefruits in groves. There was tumbleweed blowing down the main street of sad settlements on the prairies. There was the line across the sky which became the Rocky Mountains and amongst these we found Cripple

Creek, not quite a ghost town because we saw an old woman in Victorian black bent over a vegetable patch. We sailed out of New York harbour at midnight.

And I wanted the journeying never to stop. Prostitutes bought us drinks in a café at three in the morning in Antwerp. I slept with the cows in Denmark and the farmer's wife gave us cheese, rye bread and coffee for breakfast. Slept under a bandstand in Bergen, Norway and tried not to giggle as a couple coupled unaware they weren't alone. Back across to the North Sea, back to school and further dreams of escape.

## Mike Leigh film director

After the A6 Murder, for which James Hanratty was hanged, my father tried to dissuade me from hitching up north. "I'll give you the rail fare", he'd say. But I took no notice. Apart from its cheapness, hitch-hiking was a gas.

## George Monbiot journalist
### 'Goodbye Carmageddon – The perils and pleasures of ten years without a car'

This month, I think I'll have a party. I will commission a cake in the shape of a mangled vehicle. For I have something special to celebrate. Ten years ago I took one of the best decisions I have ever made. I got rid of my car. I passed my driving test when I was eighteen and bought a decrepit Renault 8 for fifty pounds, principally because I was assured that a car of this make won the Monte Carlo rally some twenty years before. I scarcely knew what to do, but I had a licence to do it, and I soon began to terrorise the neighbourhood. An ugly gang of us – farmhands, mechanics and pump attendants - began organising illegal rallies. We would scream around the country roads in the dead of night, often spinning out of control, narrowly missing other cars. It was electrifying and terrifying. One of my friends rolled his car at eighty when I was his passenger. The machine was scrunched into a ball, but both of us walked from the wreckage unscathed. A society which allows adolescents to drive on public roads is a society which has no concern for human life. Only when I became old enough to see the world from other people's point of view did I begin to slow down. As the horror of what I might have done began to grip me, I started driving less like a young man and more like a granny. I stuck resolutely to the speed limit, as a result of which I was often tailgated and abused. Car ownership became ever harder to reconcile with the rest of my life. As I earned very little, the car swallowed a great lump of my income. I discovered that it is impossible to purchase motor fuel ethically. Those oil companies not running ships aground on fragile coasts or trading with the Burmese junta are poisoning the Gulf of Mexico, prising open the Ecuadorean rainforests, or abetting the murders of trades unionists and tribal people in Colombia and Nigeria. I did not want to take part in this trade but, owning wheels, I had no choice. So, in September 1989, I took my last car, a Ford Escort even more battered and decrepit than the old Renault 8, to meet its unmakers. I walked away from the scrapyard weighed down with apprehension. I had, I believed, become a second-class citizen, stuck in the slow lane of life as the rest of the world roared past me. But I soon began to notice several unexpected effects. I realised that I had been carrying a car load of anxiety around, worrying about breakdowns, break-ins, finding a parking space or failing an MOT. I started to become more patient and less aggressive: the car had colonised my soul, shutting me off from other people, forcing me to see them only as obstacles. I began to wake up, noticing the little things I had never seen before, smelling the world, meeting people every time I travelled. And every day I found myself becoming stronger and fitter. Using an over-powered invalid carriage to get around, I had slowly been turning into an invalid.

Cycling long distances was, at first, an appalling prospect, but gradually I began to venture further afield. Now, as long as I can get my bike onto a train or a bus, almost everywhere in Britain has, once more, become accessible to me. If you add up all the time it takes to earn the money to run a car, drivers achieve an average speed of just eleven miles per hour. As I ride at an average of fourteen, and pay next to nothing, my bicycle is faster than your car.

But I must pay for my decision not to destroy the planet in other ways. Forced to use a public transport system, which is both the world's most expensive and the developed world's least efficient, I have come to see that the government, despite its protestations, simply doesn't care about the thirty two per cent of British households without access to a car. Refusing, so far, to legislate, it remains officially committed both to reducing car use and to increasing car ownership. It resolves this absurdity, every time, in favour of Middle England. Sometimes I can stand the indignities of public transport no longer, and try to hitch-hike instead. Having taken the advice of Viz magazine's Top Tips ('Hitch-hikers: improve your chances of getting a lift by not dressing up as a hunt saboteur and waving half a cardboard box at passing motorists') I stand in a lay-by hoping to exploit private transport's preposterous over-capacity. I find myself enduring a sort of psychological stoning, as drivers hurl their hostility and contempt at me: no one, they are thinking, stands by the side of the road today unless he is a scrounger, an idler or a rapist. When someone finally takes pity on me, I find myself, to my disgust, pathetically grateful. I want to explain that, far from being a favour, a lift is the least that drivers owe to non-drivers. It's everyone's planet, and they are freeloading on my decision not to mess it up. But I am never quite brave enough to do so. When there are no alternatives, I will hire a car or a van: this happens about five or six times a year. I don't enjoy it, but at least I can choose the model which suits my purpose best, and if something goes wrong, it's someone else's problem. But, above all, losing my car has encouraged me to reduce my need to travel. I used to drive for hours just to go walking in the countryside, with the result that I came back more stressed than I was before. Forced to explore nearer to home, I have found scores of wonderful and secret places. I have had to stop shopping in superstores. Buying my food from local shops, a co-operative wholesaler and an organic box scheme, I've found myself, once again, becoming both healthier and wealthier. I have begun to feel that I belong to my town and its surroundings and that they, in a small way, now belong to me.

None of this has completely dispelled the impression that I am, officially, a second class citizen. I no longer participate in the cannibal feast, but I still have to pay for it. Vehicles, according to the British Lung Foundation, cost the country some forty six billion pounds a year, while motoring taxes reap just one third of this amount. Cars sprawl across the pavement outside my house, and their alarms wake me in the middle of the night. As a pedestrian and a cyclist I am far more vulnerable than those who endanger me. Cars choke me while I'm waiting for the bus, and they force that bus to become as inefficient as they are. I will suffer just as much as drivers will if the global climate change they are hastening brings the Gulf Stream to a halt. But despite all this I remain a free man, while millions of others are held captive by their cars. Losing my car would have been much harder had I not been able-bodied or if I worked far from home or had children. Some parents in my neighbourhood go to extraordinary lengths not to be forced into cars: one family of five rides a tandem with two toddler seats and a trailer. But individuals simply cannot solve structural, institutional problems, and the car will continue to rule our lives until the government intervenes. Why is it that doing what we know to be right is always so hard, while doing what we know to be wrong is so much easier?

# Tony Hawks comedian and author

One of the great joys of hitching is the unpredictability of it all. One simply cannot say what time one will arrive anywhere – if indeed one will arrive at all. In a world where we are increasingly required to plan our days, our months, our years – not to mention making provisions for our retirement – it can be a wonderful release to cast all that dreadful 'responsibility' aside and to embrace the unknown. Furthermore, hitching happens to be an incredible 'sociable' activity in which to partake, both as lift donor and lift recipient. If someone has space in a car and is going the same way as a fellow citizen, in what way does it serve our society for that car to drive on past? In my view, more people should stop for hitch-hikers. We'd need fewer cars, there'd be less traffic and less pollution. Yes, there's the off chance that the hitcher might turn out to be a maniacal killer – but hey, sometimes you've got to live a little (or, in a worse case scenario, die a little).

My first experience of hitching was as a nineteen-year-old in America, where my obliviousness to the danger had made me somehow immune to it. On one triumphant day, I made it from Niagara Falls to New York City in a quicker time than it took the Greyhound bus. One of the drivers, seeing that I was hungry, insisted on buying me a huge lunch even though I had said that I was on a tight budget and wanted to make do with a sandwich. When I thanked him for his kindness, he simply said 'Pass it on.' I liked this selfless concept – repay me by rewarding someone else entirely with a generous dollop of goodwill.

The only slightly dodgy hitching experience I had was in France when I was picked up by an elderly man whose second question to me was what did I think of nude bathing? My immediate thought was 'pervert', and, having originally said I was headed for Lyons, I immediately revised my destination and requested that he let me off in Chalon-sur-Saone. Fortunately he assented, and I was spared further discussions of male nudity and any demonstrations which may have been required.

Obviously the best kind of hitching to be done is with a companion. In my case, in May 1997, I chose a small refrigerator. I spent one joyous month hitching my way around the circumference of Ireland with this 'cool' buddy – and I had nothing but good experiences. Furthermore, the book which I then went on to write on the subject has now sold more than half a million copies worldwide.

So don't scoff at hitching. There's more to it than just saving on the petrol.

## Amy Wislocki  editor of *Decanter* magazine

My relationship with hitch-hiking is complicated. I have never done it. I am not a big risk taker by nature – though I wish I was – and was brought up to regard it as a hazardous enterprise, especially for young blondes with a relatively sheltered upbringing. Looking back this seems rather ironic as I wouldn't be here today if it wasn't for a more liberated attitude towards the practice. Back in the freer spirited days of 1969, my mother and a friend hitched a lift on the road to North Wales. In the car was my father, and a climbing friend. The rest is history. They have now been married thirty-four years (they didn't waste much time – less than six months, in fact – another sign of how much more conservative today's betrothed tend to be).

In a sense, it would have been rather poetic if I had met a grisly end hitch-hiking. A kind of ring cycle. I would prefer to die in my sleep though.

## Gabriel Morris  for more information on the author, visit his website at gabrielmorris.bravehost.com

### 'Don't Push the Road'

I first started my lifelong fascination with hitch-hiking and consequently, adventure travel, at the intrepid age of eight. I lived with my family in the woods of Northern California, about five miles outside of a small town. Every afternoon, the school bus would drop me off at the bottom of our dirt road. From there it was another mile and a half to our big cabin in the woods and (thanks to my Dad's assertions that it would build character) it was up to my short little legs to get me home from there.

One sunny spring day, while walking home along the quiet dirt road amongst the rustling trees and melodious birdsong, I had something of a revelation. A car rolled by and kicked up a cloud of dust for me to inhale as I trudged along, building my character, but I didn't much enjoy it. I thought to myself: why am I walking this long way home every day, when I could just get a ride from someone headed in the same direction?

Twenty-two years later, I've hitch-hiked tens of thousands of miles, through every Western state, Alaska, Hawaii, the length of the United Kingdom, and a few other odd corners of the globe. I have something of a love/hate relationship with adventure travel. It can be nerve-wracking and disillusioning at times; at others incredibly thrilling, even enlightening. Once you push off that solid shore, you're at the mercy of the cosmic flow.

There are, of course, many different modes of travel. If one has the monetary resources, they can follow a fixed itinerary, taking deluxe buses from one plush hotel

room to another, eating in the fanciest restaurants – seeing the foreign culture through a series of windows, not unlike a succession of TV screens. I don't mean to knock this form of travel too much – if this is how a person likes to experience the world, then that's their business.  I doubt if I'll be hitch-hiking when I'm sixty-five.  Maybe I'll even be the one sitting back in an air-conditioned bus, on the way to a spa resort, reading about some young sprite out exploring the world for me.

However, this doesn't do much for me in my current hunger for real learning and experience.  I want the adventure, I want the challenge, I want the mystery of not knowing quite what's going to happen.  I guess this is the distinction between 'going on vacation' and 'hitting the road.'  When you hit the road, or leap into a foreign culture on their level, anything can happen – and it probably will.  If you're willing to put your soul out there, go along for the ride and brave the unknown, you'll undoubtedly have encounters that will change your mind, like nothing else can.

There's an old proverb told by river boatmen – "Don't push the river."  In short, there's no point in trying to control the flow of something that is undoubtedly beyond your control.  Instead of simply muscling something to do your bidding, go with the flow, work with it instead of against it—and learn what it has to teach in the process.

This same approach can be applied to travel.  Call it the Tao of Travel, or the Zen, or the Art, or whatever you like.  Getting that perfect ride: meeting that strange, enlightening character who reveals the mysterious, foreign world around you; or manoeuvring through a challenging situation that seems to have no easy resolution – these can be lessons in both personal power and faith.  You can see the churning rapids up ahead, yet you know you're going to ride through it and not be taken under, because you're in touch with the flow around you.  You can see the car coming, and you sense that this person is going to pick you up, rearrange your view of reality, and then drop you off somewhere you otherwise never would have found yourself.  You are in a state of surrender, yet simultaneously in control of your destiny.

I can't even count the times in which I've been stuck on the side of the road as the sun is going down, only halfway to my destination after a long and frustrating day of hitch-hiking.  And yet, more often than not – just as I'm beginning to despair, preparing myself psychologically to hike off into the woods and spend an unpleasant night curled up under some bush – someone comes along and delivers me to a warm bed, whether it be mine or theirs (or more likely, their couch).

In an instant, I go from cursing the whole damn universe to a state of gratitude – humanity has redeemed itself, thanks to one kind-hearted person.  Oftentimes, the most profound travelling experiences take place when you're out on that proverbial limb and it appears to be cracking; you're at the edge of desperation, wondering if you can hold on much longer; you're faced with the great unknown, no idea how it's all going to work out this time, no plan for getting yourself through this one. And yet that simple twist of fate comes along, and pretty soon you're riding high again, cruising on down the road. The river spat you out; the rapids are behind you.

There's a certain thrill to hitch-hiking because of its erratic nature. You might stand there on the side of the road for hours, even days. Or someone might pull over before you've even had the chance to set your pack down. You might get a ride a half mile down the road, leaving you in a terrible spot that you'll have to spend time and energy hiking out of. Or you might get a ride from someone who'll take you all the way across the country. You might get a ride from someone with such a terrible disposition, you're left wondering, "What in the world compelled this person to pick me up anyway?" Or you might get picked up by someone who'll turn out to be a lifelong friend. You just never know what the hell is going to happen. And that's the real beauty of it. That's what adventure is all about. That's what learning about the world is all about—because you can't truly learn, without challenging your mind to stretch beyond its self-imposed constraints. And you can't do that without letting go of a certain amount of control, and simply trusting that the wind, or the river, or the road, is on its way to somewhere that's worth checking out – and that one way or another, it'll most likely get you there.

## Lars Therkildsen historian

In the mid-1990s, my companion and I travelled across Eastern Europe by train, because the hitching had been thin on the ground. When we reached Budapest we were finally able to take up hitch-hiking again. Despite a two-hour wait for a lift, we soon reached Vienna and, a few days later, Prague – two cities of great beauty. We met a lot of pleasant and interesting people on the road who told us about themselves and their countries. In this respect, hitch-hiking is a great way to travel. We learned some tricks: we found out by accident, that if the driver was a bit shy and silent it only sufficed to mention the words "foreigners" and "immigrants" and then – since everyone has an opinion on this subject – they wouldn't stop talking, and you just had to put in "yes" and "no" at the appropriate places and nod regularly.

# Remy Chevalier   editor-at-large ElectrifyingTimes.com
## 'Roads Are Like Rivers, Cars Are Like Boats'

Roads are like rivers and cars are like boats... There is an unwritten code of the sea, where a fellow traveller in need is always welcome aboard. So why doesn't this apply to land? It used to... If you were walking down a deserted road 'in the old days' and a stage coach happened by, they'd have given you a ride, wouldn't they?

Today, if you stick your thumb out on the street, people just look at you like you're crazy. There's only two reasons why anybody would hitch today. Either your car broke down and you don't have a cell phone to call a cab, or you're flat broke. Only 'hippies' hitch in the USA. But it got me around.

I landed in the USA in the early seventies to escape the French authorities who wanted to drop kick my little white ass in jail for military service evasion. I wanted to serve my planet, not just one country! I ended up penniless in Hollywood hob-knobbing with the upcoming crop of new science fiction visionaries, desperately trying to insert environmental themes into storylines. They became billionaires, I'm still begging for food!

Hitch-hiking in LA was easy, because I'd get picked up by gays on the prowl who just assumed I was a male prostitute. I'd fend them off by endlessly talking about pollution. It got me to where I was going. I had a couple of close calls, but I was a skinny 6'3" and nobody dared mess with me.

I wasn't always car-less mind you. In the three years I lived in LA, I had wheels most of the time. But they were old wrecks I'd buy for $200 and drive around till the day came to head for the junk yard. The big white Cadi with fins I drove around LA for months, in midnight chases with the cops down Sunset Boulevard, got a lot of attention. The day I drove it down to the junk yard with smoking brake pads on fire, the producers of *The Deer Hunter* were there waiting. I got $75 for it. My ol' Cadi is now immortalized on screen, fat dent in the door I put there and all.

I loved that car. It had a huge front seat you could slide over. One late night I took a lone ride down Malibu. Two hippie chicks were hitch-hiking in the dead of night, so silly me, I picked them up. I apologized for driving a gas guzzler, explaining I'd wish we could find a clean source of power, like the UFOs do. In my rear view mirror I caught a glimpse of the girl in the back seat fiddling with a switch blade. I asked her what that was for, oblivious to their intentions. She said they had planned on killing me but that I turned out to be a nice guy. Years later I realized they had probably been Manson girls.

You meet wonderful people hitch-hiking. It's an adventure. Even when I had a car in LA, I would hitch cross country to save gas and money. I'd head East to Florida to visit my folks. It would take me about three days catching truckers. One of them greeted me by pulling a .44 Magnum from his arm rest and pointed it straight at my nose, telling me not to give him any trouble. He then went on to reminisce about his wrestling days as Mr. X.

One time a trucker who used to live in Connecticut gave me a ride. He knew an architect in Baton Rouge he thought I should meet. We went to his house and they showed me this light box with the drawing of a black triangular building he was planning for IBM in downtown Westport. I thought they were pulling my leg. It looked so dark and ominous. A couple of years later I learned it was to be headquarters to the UPC symbol, you know, the bar code on everything you buy? But it was never built, because the Internet happened and made the need for a big brother computer obsolete.

Hitch-hiking ain't safe, but it could save the planet. It just needs to be made safe. There's ways of doing that. You can call it 'slugging' if you want, but it's still hitch-hiking. Imagine how many cars we could get off the road, and the fuel we could save, if people weren't terrified to give each other a ride? That's why we need to institutionalise hitching.

A group in California is doing just that. They call themselves GoGeronimo. I found out about them after I'd drafted my own plan for Lü magazine. The idea is simple. Make hitch-hiking into a National Club, with big laminated photo IDs. The IDs are interchangeable for both drivers and riders. Drivers display it on their windshield and riders wear it around their neck. The IDs are awarded by the DMV or police stations, where they run a security check and keep your name on file. The card would have a bar code to scan on the spot, online or by cell phone, to make sure you're not a serial rapist.

That means in the morning, when America goes to work, instead of taking your car into a sea of grid lock, you can simply walk outside your door and flag down a ride from a fellow card holder, and vice versa. That's what is starting to happen in Washington DC where 'slugging' is slowly replacing car pooling. It's OK to stand out there with your briefcase in one hand and a cup of coffee in the other. It's O-K!

I don't hitch much anymore, because I'm getting too old, too lazy, but also because I live in a filthy rich part of the country where spoiled high school jocks love to throw empty beer cans at your head. But I still do it once in awhile when my broken down Subaru is in the shop. And I always meet someone interesting, or rediscover an old friend I hadn't seen in years.

Hitch-hiking is good. It rekindles community. It brings people together. It saves resources. If I could simply step out of my house and hitch a ride to go down town, I would. But right now I know I'd be there for a few hours before a neighbour took pity on me. This can change. We can change it. We need to change it. We need to make hitch-hiking a part of our daily lifestyle, and make it safe so Jim Morrison can wink and giggle back at us from his hut deep in the African tundra.

## James Hobbs journalist

Hitch-hiking began for me in the late-1970s when I was in my late teens, and looking back it was an essential part of becoming independent and leaving home. You take risks, you meet people, you go places. Living in semi-rural Devon it was usually the quickest way to travel and always the cheapest. Quicker than buses, certainly, that usually came several days after you needed them.

My elder brother encouraged me in this, if not my parents. He had a copy of *Hitch-Hikers' Manual* by Simon Calder, which offered useful information on how to get around Britain. In the summer of 1982 my mate Graham and I hitch-hiked across France to the coast. We fled south with often terrifying speed – contradicting Calder's warning: "France – slow, police bad". But no system of queuing or hitching etiquette was apparent – we spent the best part of a week on a heavily-populated slip road, and it was only the sight of us lying on the verge with our thumbs outstretched and hats over our eyes that caught someone's eye and made them take pity on us.

One of the great things about hitch-hiking, of course, is that you are never sure who you are going to get to meet. I've been picked up by everyone from members of parliament to pig farmers, who were both preferable to a friend who hitched a lift from someone who evidently had a drink problem. Things were going well until the driver started drinking from a newly opened bottle of whisky as he drove. He offered it to his passenger, who realised that the more of it he could consume, the more likely they were to arrive at their destination without having an accident. The opportunity to drink to save your life doesn't come along too often, and is one to be embraced.

## Gabe Quirk

After reading a few Kerouac books, looking at photos of far-off places in America, and just wanting to have an 'experience' I decided to stick out my thumb and see what would happen. And within 5 minutes I had a ride in a brand new sedan cruising through the northern California forests.

Most of my hitching experiences have been in the western US. It seems that people here are more laid back and friendly in general. Also, since there are fewer towns they are usually going farther than someone in the east would be. Half the time the drivers end up offering more than just a ride – no, I'm not talking about sex – I'm talking about food, a place to sleep, and even some money. I've accepted the first two, but money isn't needed, people just think it is. Most of my rides have been with middle-aged white men. I've had rides from some females though. One lady even told me that she had just been shot in the head three months before and she figured if that didn't kill her I wouldn't either. I've never had an uncomfortable, scary feeling about the drivers after hopping in their car. Nothing but positive interactions with people who at first are strangers, and within five minutes are friends.

I really think that people, especially Americans, need to realize that the vast majority of people on this blue orb are nice and have good intentions. On the nightly news we constantly hear about murders, rapes, robberies, etc. But in a country with 285 million people, there are billions of good deeds being performed each and every day. And on a planet with 6.2 billion people, there are billions of good deeds going on right now.

# Good Trips

# David Nobbs  novelist and scriptwriter
## 'A Hitch-Hiker's Summer in Europe'

I hitched round Europe with my friends Chris and Sally in 1957. It was a trip that began and ended with memorable lifts, but there were some strange moments in between. Chris and I met up in Bavaria and hitched to Milan to meet Sally.

We got to Innsbruck without difficulty, our last lift being from a delightful young German doctor and his pretty wife. They had been married for two whole days.

I don't think I could have been so sociable on my honeymoon.

We had dreadful trouble leaving Innsbruck via the Brenner Pass. There was nothing but holiday traffic, laden with luggage, boats, dinghies, water skis and grannies. We stood there for nine hours. Our legs ached. Our thumbs throbbed. Nobody stopped.

Next day we couldn't face standing in the same spot. We caught a train to the Italian border. Same result. After four hours we returned to the station to catch a train to Vipiteno, where we might pick up some local traffic. There wasn't a train for an hour.

"Come on." I said. "Let's go back and try till the train's due."

Back to the road we trudged. The very first car that came by was the cheery VW of our honeymoon couple. They stopped with broad smiles, and took us all the way to Merano by a stunningly spectacular mountain route.

In Merano they dropped us outside their hotel and said, "Be here at eleven tomorrow. We'll take you to Milan."

On the way to Milan we stopped for a drink on a terrace beside Lake Como. It was a breathtakingly beautiful scene. An English coach party arrived, and a rather unattractive English girl jumped on a table and shouted, "I'm in Italy." Chris and I cringed.

"Don't worry," said our German friend in his impeccable if slightly formal English. "Our compatriots have given us much cause for embarrassment over the years."

During the next weeks we toured Liguria, Tuscany and Umbria and rarely had to wait more than half an hour for a lift. Our worst lift? Three come to mind.

There was the one in the white van. "Perugia?" we asked.

"Si si," came the encouraging reply. Imagine our disappointment when after four hundred yards the van turned right into a housing estate and rang its chimes. It was an ice cream van.

Then there was the lorry. Sally was extremely attractive, and one lorry driver stopped on a lonely stretch of road and said to Chris and me, "You - out. She – stay."

He grabbed hold of Sally. Somehow we managed to get her free from him without hurting her, but it wasn't a pleasant moment. But the third and most dangerous lift was the one where our driver was overtaken by a Jag. What humiliation. The next forty kilometres of the picturesque winding road between Siena and Florence were absolutely terrifying as our driver sought to satisfy Italian honour in front of his English passengers. We got to Florence exhausted, alive – just – and ahead of the Jag.

In a bar in Bologna the proprietress admired Sally's beauty. "Bella architectura." There's a lot of *bella architectura* in Bologna but Sally's won us free drinks all night and a lift arranged for the next day from a very willing Italian businessman.

One lift came with the offer of free accommodation in the driver's barn. We slept well on that balmy summer night, drifting to sleep on a lullaby of owls.

Our second memorable trip was in our second VW. This was driven by a German racing driver who had competed several times in the famous Italian road race, the Mille Miglie.

Halfway up the autobahn, he said, "I hate these things. So many rules. One thing you are not allowed to do is this", and he swung the little VW right over the grass of the central reservation into the opposite carriageway, drove south for several miles, then did the same thing again and resumed his journey to Mannheim.

In Ludwigshafen, opposite Mannheim on the Rhine, the police offered us free accommodation in the wartime bunkers under the city. We spent a bizarre night in those narrow, yellow tunnels. In the morning, the police found us a lift on a Rhine barge. There was only one snag. The bargee had died on Tuesday, and it was a funeral procession. We would have to wear black armbands and remain silent. We declined. We had some sensitivity.

In Holland we stayed at a youth hostel in a village where the only restaurant was closed due to a wedding. How could we eat? Easy. We were invited to a wedding. I hope that would happen to a Dutch couple stranded in an English village. It was a lovely experience.

In Rotterdam, Chris and Sally raised hitching to an art form by thumbing a lift on a passing tramp steamer.

I decided to go on north to Copenhagen. The previous summer, I had sailed round Denmark but bad weather had prevented us reaching the capital.

I took a bus to Breda, on the outskirts of the Rotterdam conurbation. After half an hour a car pulled up and I noticed DK on the back. A Dane! I didn't dare ask for Copenhagen straight off. I said I wanted to go to Nijmegen, where I had arranged a poste restante facility.

"Is your poste restante very important?" he asked as we approached Nijmegen, I having by now admitted that eventually I was going to Copenhagen.

"Not very," I said.

We slept that night in his car in the forests of Germany. In the morning the car wouldn't start. While we waited for a repair vehicle, we had a Westphalische Fruhstuck (ham, eggs, cheese, pumpernickel, coffee and schnapps) at a local inn. Fabulous.

On the slip road to the autobahn outside Bremen, in our repaired car, we stopped to pick up another youth.

"Him. He has a tent," said our driver.

The very polite Dutch boy with the very large tent said he was going to Hamburg, but when our driver stopped for petrol he admitted that he was actually aiming for Copenhagen. "Do I have to get out at Hamburg?" he asked me.

"Stay put," I advised. "I was only going to Nijmegen."

There was no mention of stopping until we got to a camp site near the Danish border. "I'll buy food," said our driver. "You have cooking equipment with your tent?"

We dined magnificently *al fresco*, slept well in the huge tent, and set off gently the next morning.

"We take lunch at my brother's. He is a farmer," said the driver.

After a delicious and substantial Danish farmhouse lunch, we were driven in state to Copenhagen, where our driver enquired, "Now, which evening would suit you boys best to come for dinner and meet my wife?"

One lift all the way from Rotterdam to Copenhagen, with two free nights and four free meals! I didn't hitch much after that. I wanted to end at the top.

Oh, those innocent hitch-hiking days of long ago.

## Arnold Wesker  playwright/director

My last memory of hitching was when I was heading for Glasgow with a couple of friends to take part in a concert given by a Jewish choir of which I was a member. We were ahead of time, which was just as well because we got stuck in Berwick-on-Tweed. I suggested we go to a police station to ask if we could stay for the night. They offered us a couple of cells, gate left open, and made us eggs and bacon for breakfast. It was not an orthodox Jewish choir!!

## Stephen R. Bissette  24 years in the American comic book industry
(as a cartoonist, writer, editor, publisher, and co-publisher), best-known for *Saga of the Swamp Thing*, *Taboo*, *'1963'*, *Tyrant*, and more. http://www.comicon.com/bissette

I was stranded, trying to get from Montpelier to a place in Bethel I'd been invited to, the home of Vincent Fago, a grand old comic artist and children's book illustrator. As luck had it, the truck driver who picked me up in Montpelier was a talkative and outgoing soul, and oddly enough he knew just the place I was hoping to get to. I wasn't too comfortable with his directions, but he insisted, letting me off on Interstate 89 before the Bethel exit, where a dirt road cut over the interstate and into the woods on the right, heading south.

He pulled over and pointed and said, "Listen, I wouldn't steer you wrong. Listen to me now: walk up that road, cuts right betwixt a barn and a house, and don't you mind the dogs, they won't bite, and just keep walking about a quarter-mile, and you'll be right t'where yer goin'."

I thanked him, and took my backpack and lifted my art folio out of the back of his truck.

He said, "Good luck, young fella, and tell Vince I said hi," and drove off.

He hadn't steered me wrong. That back road indeed passed between a farm and a worn old farmhouse, dogs and all, and sure enough just a short autumn day walk from there I was at the home of Vince Fago, vet cartoonist extraordinaire, who was on the roof of his porch sweeping off leaves. We'd never met before but I did have an invite, and it was a visit that changed my work and my life for the better. So, you see, my one hitch-hiking experience as the one thumbing a ride was a blessed one. When I put out the light that night in the guest room at the Fago home, I thanked that truck-driver before I lay down in a big saggy-mattress bed, and drifted off to sleep.

# Gareth Rees writer, artist, musician

I was heading back with others to England from the Middle East, first travelling by boat to Rijeka, near the Italian border and then hitch-hiking past Venice. It never occurred to us to take the opportunity to visit Venice on this occasion as it could somehow suck money. A cup of coffee in such a place might cost the equivalent of two days' worth of food.

We got stuck at nightfall in Rimini. The police ordered us to a camp site. We didn't want nor could afford a camp site but the police escorted us anyway.

We didn't have a tent, didn't want one. By this time we'd gotten to enjoy uninterrupted views of the stars. In a parched place meant for a tent, we laid out our sleeping bags and went to sleep. Waking in the morning, all around was camp activity. Children playing, people cooking or eating breakfast. We were sandwiched between two tents containing German families. I don't know if our open-to-the-world, tentless state made them sorry for us. Whatever, these two families ensured we had a very, very good breakfast.

# Dave Unwin editor *Today's Pilot*

As night began to fall across the Tanami Desert it began to occur to me that, as hot as the day had been, the night was going to be equally cold. Trust me to get a lift in an open-top Landrover!

I remember it all as if it were yesterday. I was twenty-one years old and looking forward to the trip of a lifetime. I'd been working hard down the Scheelite mine on King Island in the Bass Strait, and saved up a lot of money. Now I was looking forward to spending it. With my good mates Bellini and JJ, who'd also been at the mine, I hitched northwards out of Melbourne on a glorious March day, nursing a king-size hangover. The next six weeks would see the three of us involved in several amusing (and at times unbelievable) escapades! We'd decided to split up, on the grounds that it would be much easier to get lifts singly, with a vague agreement that we'd meet up in Darwin sometime in May. As events transpired, I was to meet up with both of them (sometimes simultaneously) on the long hitch north.

The first event to really stick in my mind was when I was picked up by a pan-fried old yeti near the New South Wales-Queensland border. I was never able to ascertain exactly what he did, but for all I know he may well have been a professional stoner.

Anyway, almost before I'd got my seatbelt on he'd produced a huge joint, made from a particularly powerful strain of marijuana known as 'Mullumbimbi madness', after a town in New South Wales that was populated almost entirely by hippies. This was my first exposure to what is probably best described as 'weapons grade' dope, and when the old yeti dropped me off in a small hick town in the middle of nowhere I was a flurbling, gerbling wreck. When I got out of the car I realised that I could hardly stand! I barely knew who I was; I certainly didn't know where I was, or when it was. In fact, about the only thing I did know with any real certainty was that I really didn't want to get into a car with someone I didn't know! Finally, after a protracted period of sitting in the shade of a large Eucalyptus tree while struggling to get my shit together I swore that, no matter what, I wouldn't make that mistake again!

Having hooked up with Bellini and JJ in Townsville for a week of serious drinking and sunbathing, we split up again and headed west, towards the mining town of Mount Isa. After a protracted wait, I eventually got a lift with three young blokes in an ancient Holden of dubious roadworthiness. After we'd got through the introductions, I was just telling them about Bellini and JJ when who should we see standing by the side of the road and thumbing vigorously but Bellini! Good lads that they were, the boys stopped, Bellini got in and we continued on our way. Needless to say, about a few hours later a familiar figure loomed out of the heat haze… JJ! Caught up in the spirit of the moment, the boys sportingly offered JJ a ride. The rickety old Holden was now distinctly overloaded, yet curiously it didn't seem to occur to anyone that grossly overloading such a knackered old car wasn't the world's greatest idea. We were soon to have this lesson brought home to all of us in a very exciting way…

The rear wheel had been making some rather peculiar noises for some time but, devoid of all mechanical sympathy, we'd chosen to deal with it by turning the radio up. With hindsight, this probably wasn't the most productive idea, and a little bit of preventive maintenance would have been a lot more useful. Anyway, the poor old wheel eventually decided that enough was enough, and indicated its extreme displeasure at the abuse we were heaping upon it by suddenly parting company with the axle! Well, after what seemed like several minutes of serious fear as the car lurched from one side of the road to another while trailing an impressive shower of sparks, the Holden finally ground to a halt. We all got out, congratulated ourselves on what had been a very narrow squeak, and then walked back down the road looking for the wheel! Eventually Bellini, JJ and I tired of this, wished the boys well and set off west again, trudging through swarms of flies and clouds of dust into the setting sun.

I have no clear recollection of exactly where we were when the wheel fell off, but I do recall the hitching being a bit lean. We split up, then a few days later I ran back into

Bellini and we got stuck on the edge of the desert in a real one-horse town. In fact it was worse than that, as the horse had recently died! In desperation, we tried to jump one of the freight trains that occasionally passed through, but the bastard driver saw us lurking and speeded up before we could get aboard.

Eventually an open-topped Landrover appeared through the clouds of dust and flies, crewed by two blokes and a large (but luckily friendly) Alsatian. We drove right across the Tanami Desert in this vehicle, being alternately roasted during the day and frozen at night. I remember mentioning to Bellini, "This will make a good story, someday."

Eventually we got to Darwin and, as agreed, Bellini and I made our way to a large campsite on the outskirts of the city. As we looked for somewhere to pitch our tents, the familiar figure of JJ appeared, trudging slowly through the dust. Incredibly, after hitching literally thousands of miles over six weeks, we all arrived at the RV within hours of each other!

# Rachel Crabtree

I left Calais where I'd been stuck for a week with no money. Some shitty things happened at first; some gendarme pointing a gun at me for taking water from the camp site next door – there was a big campsite by the beach at Calais – caravans and all that. But next to it, outside the fence, was the beach and all the travellers used to go there because you didn't have to pay, of course, and these slanging matches would go on through the wire.

Anyway, at this time there were a lot of people sleeping on the beach – some, like the Danish, had tents but most were just there with sleeping bags and travelling light. Every night there was a party of some sort, everyone gravitated to a fire by the sea and most people brought dope or wine and there was always some food – lentils or something – and there was this Spanish guy who could play guitar really nicely, and he was singing and then he asked if anyone had any requests. So some Italian asked for an Italian folk song and this guy knew it and he sang and the Italians were very impressed. And so this Greek asked if he knew this particular Greek song. And sure enough he knew it – and so it went on – strange Norwegian songs, German, whatever – he seemed to know them all.

And I guess because of the dope and things it became weirder and weirder and this guy began to scare people – I didn't even ask him if he knew 'Blaydon Races' because he probably did!

THE FOLLOWING IS AN EXCERPT FROM A 72-PAGE TRAVEL DIARY COMIC BOOK. AT THIS POINT IN THE STORY I'M ON MY WAY BACK HOME (TO NEW YORK) AFTER SEVEN WEEKS OF TRAVELLING EUROPE. WITH A COMBINATION OF HITCH-HIKING AND TRAINS (AND ONE PAID "RIDESHARE") I'D GONE SOUTH FROM LONDON TO SPAIN, EAST TO ROMANIA, NORTH TO POLAND, AND WEST TO GERMANY. THE DATE IS MONDAY, NOVEMBER 29TH, 1999 (I'D RECENTLY TURNED 24). I'M IN FRANKFURT, GERMANY, AND I'VE MADE UP MY MIND TO HITCH THE REST OF THE WAY BACK WEST.

TIME TO START HITCH-HIKING AGAIN.

A RIDESHARE OFFICE! MIGHT AS WELL TAKE A LOOK BEFORE I GO.

A TURN OF EVENTS...

ACTUALLY, WE HAVE A RIDE GOING TO KÖLN LEAVING IN FIVE MINUTES FOR ONLY A FEW DOLLARS.

HMM, FROM THERE IT WOULD BE EASY TO HITCH WEST... AND EASIER THAN FINDING MY WAY OUT OF YET ANOTHER CITY ON FOOT.

I'LL TAKE IT.

THE DRIVER WAS A GOOD-LOOKING GERMAN WOMAN. THE TWO OTHER RIDERS AND MYSELF ALL LOADED UP OUR SMALL COLLECTION OF POSSESSIONS AND WITHIN TEN MINUTES WE WERE OFF.

IT WAS A VERY PLEASANT RIDE, ON A FINE SUNNY DAY. THE GUY IN BACK WITH ME FELL ASLEEP,...

...BUT I HAD GOOD CONVERSATIONS WITH THE MAN IN THE FRONT SEAT. HE WAS FROM GHANA, AFRICA, AND HAD MOVED TO GERMANY TEN YEARS AGO.

TO PEOPLE WHO SAY THEY FEAR TO VISIT AFRICA, I SAY "COME TO AFRICA! SEE AFRICA! SEE GHANA! THEN MAKE UP YOUR MIND."

PEOPLE IN EUROPE AND AMERICA THINK THERE IS MUCH FIGHTING IN AFRICA, MANY GUNS...BUT WHO SOLD THEM THE GUNS? AND THEY DO NOT REALIZE THAT AFRICA IS VERY LARGE, AND THERE ARE MANY DIFFERENT PEOPLES AND NATIONS.

WOW. YEAH, I'D LOVE TO GO...

WE ALSO SPOKE OF GERMANY'S SOCIALIZED SYSTEMS; IT WAS NICE TO GET A DIFFERENT PERSPECTIVE AFTER THE ONE I'D GOTTEN ON THE WAY TO FRANKFURT.

I DON'T UNDERSTAND. YOU MEAN IN AMERICA IF YOU GET SICK... WHAT HAPPENS?

IF YOU HAVE NO INSURANCE OR MEDICAL PLAN, YOU GOTTA PAY.

BUT WHAT IF YOU DON'T HAVE MONEY?

THEN YOU JUST HOPE YOU DON'T GET SICK!

BUT THAT IS CRAZY!

**Jeffrey Lewis** New York City comic book artist; songwriter with albums on Rough Trade Records. See www.TheJeffreyLewisSite.com

THAT DAY ALSO BROUGHT THE ONLY WEIRDO DRIVER I'D HAD STOP FOR ME... IT WAS ON A SMALL ROAD IN THE AFTERNOON. THE GUY WAS A FREAKY ANCIENT FRENCHMAN WITH JESUS PARAPHRENALIA AND LOTS OF JUNK IN HIS RAGGEDY CAR.

MAN, THERE'S CRUMBLY WAFFLE-COOKIES AND WHAT LOOKS LIKE BITS OF CHEESE ALL OVER THE PASSENGER SEAT... AND THIS GUY LOOKS TOO OLD AND FEEBLE TO BE ON THE ROAD.

HE WASN'T HEADED IN MY DIRECTION HOWEVER, SO I DIDN'T END UP GETTING IN.

ANYWAY, I DID MAKE CALAIS. WHEN MY RIDE DROPPED ME AT THE FERRY TERMINAL (THANK GOD I DIDN'T HAVE TO MAKE MY WAY THROUGH THE CITY AGAIN) THE NIGHT WAS DARK AND COLD AND WINDY. AGAIN I SOON GAVE UP TRYING TO HITCH A RIDE ONTO THE BOAT AND INSTEAD SHELLED OUT THIRTY-FIVE BUCKS FOR A TICKET.

BUT ON THE OTHER SIDE THEY SAID IT COSTS THE SAME BOTH WAYS!

WELL, IT DOESN'T.

I WOULD HAVE BOUGHT A ROUND-TRIP, BUT THEY ASSURED ME IT COST TWENTY-FOUR HERE TOO!

MAN, I'VE GOT MUCH LESS CASH THAN I THOUGHT. DIDN'T I JUST CHANGE A HUNDRED DOLLAR CHECK A COUPLE DAYS AGO? MAYBE THE EXCHANGE GUY RIPPED ME OFF?

MY GOD, I CAN'T BELIEVE I'M LEAVING EUROPE. SO LONG, EUROPE!

IT ALWAYS FEELS STRANGE TO APPROACH THE LAST LEG OF A JOURNEY. LIKE READING THE LAST CHAPTER OF A BOOK.

THE RETURN TRIP FROM THE CONTINENT WAS MUCH QUICKER AND SMOOTHER THAN THE INITIAL CROSSING HAD BEEN.

LUCKILY, THE COAST LOOKED CLEAR TO SPEND THE NIGHT ON SOME SOFT CHAIRS IN THE WAITING ROOM AFTER WE ARRIVED IN DOVER. AT FIRST I TRIED TO LOOK AS THOUGH I WAS ACTUALLY JUST WAITING, BUT AS IT BECAME OBVIOUS THAT OTHER PASSENGERS WERE LYING DOWN AND SLEEPING, AND NOBODY CARED, I TOOK OFF MY SHOES AND STRETCHED OUT.

ZZZ

I HAD MADE MUCH BETTER TIME THAN I'D EXPECTED! I HAD ONLY LEFT FRANKFURT ON MONDAY, AND THERE I WAS IN ENGLAND ON TUESDAY NIGHT!

Jeffrey Lewis New York City comic book artist; songwriter with albums on Rough Trade Records. See www.TheJeffreyLewisSite.com

# John Bartlett a sometime itinerant player and follower of Thespis!

On our last day in the West Country, our meanderings had led us to a little pub in Brixham, the name of which escapes me. However, as we were debating what to do that evening, an elderly, but sprightly lady entered for a 'swift half' before returning home with her daily shopping. It wasn't long before some friendly banter was being exchanged. She wanted to know who we were and what we were doing in Brixham. We explained that we were on a 'Grand Tour' of Devon and Cornwall and that Guy had driven, but Dave and I had hitched down. This proved to be all the encouragement she needed to tell us about her own adventures. It turned out that some fifty years or so earlier, in the 1920s, this extraordinary lady had hitched right across America, even managing to hitch a lift back to England on a passing steamer! But this was not the end of her story; eventually, after a seaboard romance, she married the captain! Toasting her success and resourcefulness, the conversation turned to the evening's entertainment. On learning about our dilemma she quickly quashed the notion of a meal and insisted that we visit 'The V & A' in Stoke Gabriel, as once a week the locals had a sing-song and tonight was the night! So be it, the die had been cast and 'The V & A' it was!

That evening, clutching a road map and torch, we set off for the elusive Stoke Gabriel. The dark, overhung, winding lanes periodically turned into 'T' junctions or crossroads and by the side of the road the white cast iron signposts helpfully guided us on our way: Stoke Gabriel 2 miles, Stoke Gabriel 3 miles or even Stoke Gabriel 4 miles! Whichever way we decided to turn, the circuitous two or three miles always seemed to remain two or three 'country miles'; however we did eventually fetch up at 'The V & A'. The promised sing-song was in full swing, with the locals singing song after song, accompanied by a jovial grey haired lady on a beaten-up piano. She played and they sang or they sang and she joined in. This arrangement suited both parties until a slightly bawdy song was chosen by the singers, whereupon the jocular grande-dame, like a demented mother hen, grasped a school hand bell and rent the air with its peels until order was resumed and a more suitable song was selected!

A magnificent evening was had by all and eventually we joyfully left the pub to wend our way home with, "Merrily we roll along, roll along, roll along" ringing in our youthful ears. That much sought-after, elusive, magical evening has never been equalled before or since! Today the pub remains, but some of the interior has been modified and altered. But, resting quietly in a forgotten corner, the piano gently gathers dust and, to the discerning eye, acts as a reminder of those wonderful musical times of yore!

The next day we all went our separate ways, an easy uneventful trip home in cars and lorries ensued, and we all met up that evening to relive again our 'great adventure'!

## Bernd Wechner committed hitch-hiker and columnist for Suite 101.com
### 'An Auspicious Ride'

I had the pleasure of working with some Ananda Marga monks on their food stall at the millennium ConFest, an alternative lifestyles festival on the Murray River in Australia. It took place in the winter of 1997 when I was hitch-hiking back from Canberra to Wollongong after a round trip of the south east of Australia. I had just got out at Bungendore, and on account of the wonderful weather and a desire to leave the village behind me, I started walking towards the coast. I hadn't walked far, was still in the village, which wasn't a kilometre long, when a car passed me by and pulled up some 100 metres ahead of me. Now this might be a ride, and it might not, and I'd seen too many naïve hitchers rush up to the parked car thrilled to bits about the ride they'd won, only to find some driver looking at them like they'd come from another planet, because the driver had only pulled over to read a map or some such thing and hadn't even noticed this freaky hitcher. That, I daresay, is one of hitching's most embarrassing moments, and if *Candid Camera* ever found enough hitchers to poke fun at, that's just what they'd do, drive past them and pull up a little ahead with the indicator on, and wait for them to rush up gushing with energy and joy only to turn them away and catch the shift of mood on film as they realised their error. And, true enough, the car ahead of me indicated and pulled out well before I got much closer. Though, hold on, it was doing a U-ey. I guessed they'd gone the wrong way, just realised, pulled over and were now doubling back. It drove past me again, and behind me threw another U-turn, to pull up just behind me! The young lady at the wheel got out and waved me over! It was, it was a ride! Now that was personal attention for you. She was going to Mogo down on the coast, so she could get me down to the coast road anyway. I'd get out at the junction to the Princes Highway, where she'd head south to Mogo and I'd head north. She didn't usually pick up hitchers, but then I looked O.K. it seems, at least from behind. She'd grown up with hitching culture mind you, on the south coast of New South Wales, where if you didn't have a car, you hitched. So the family had always taken hitchers along and she'd hitched around a bit herself. We got to talking. She was studying in Canberra and went back home to Mogo every weekend. I used to live with a guy from down that way, Broulee in fact. He was studying at Wollongong Uni, where I'd studied too. She'd studied at Wollongong for a while too before moving to Canberra. She moved because she couldn't afford the rent up in the 'Gong and had relos down in Canberra where she stayed rent-free. Well, it was around the same time that we were both last living in the 'Gong, and we weren't living far from one another, just behind the hospital there. "Hey," she said, "that guy from Broulee you lived with wasn't living there with you, was he?""Sure was ... Andrew was the name." She laughed. Of all the things. She had an old childhood friend, Andrew, who was living there at the same time. The same Andrew! Small world! Small Australia! It was auspicious. I'd meant to drop in on Andrew on the way south a month ago. Had just got his address from a mutual friend in Sydney a few days before hitting the road. But it turns out he was away in Perth on a job, where he was spending every three weeks out of four lately. This time I'd not planned a visit at all, I was just running critically low on time, having taken so long to cross the western plains of New South Wales. But here I was, picked up by a close friend of his, who now told me he was home for the weekend, and we'd just have to drop in. So she took me round to Andrew's, and true enough he was home, and got the surprise of his life to see who Michelle had picked up by the side of the road, hitching out of Bungendore! We got to talking about the trip, and the machinations of life. I'd ridden into Bungendore from Queanbeyan with a guy in a red Merc. She'd been overtaken by a red Merc with two people in it coming out of Queenbeyan! She remembered it well, she was just driving up the hill out of town, and this red Merc came racing past. But hey, if she was ahead of the Merc, she must have driven by me as I stood in Queenbeyan; why then did she pull over in Bundgendore with such intent? We'd passed her not five hundred metres from where I was standing it seemed. Turned out she'd just pulled out of a side road behind me as I was getting into this red Merc, and then we pulled out and raced past her, I was put off in Bungendore and started walking out of town, by which time she'd caught up again in time to see me ...

The machinery of life is amazing at times and we let the clock tick by, tempting the fates, throwing ourselves into the maelstrom of the unknown, in my case courting the road for all she's worth. When I think of how Michelle found me, how she picked me up, who Michelle was, where she took me, that I'd never known or heard of her beforehand and the many thousands of cars buzzing around Canberra, I have to confess to a certain awe.

# Julia Oseledeko 25-year-old great traveller and true dreamer
## 'Hitch-Hiking: Connecting People'

I'd like to tell you a story about how a hitch-hiker can become a postman. For New Year's Eve 2002 my friend and I decided to go to Abkhazia, an independent but unrecognised republic one hundred kilometres from St Petersburg. Before we left we met up with some people from Abkhazia who complained to us that there was no mail connection so they hadn't heard from their relatives for a long time. They wrote letters to their relatives saying that my friend and I were coming to Adzubzha village in Abkhazia. They also gave us their relatives' 'phone numbers.

A few days later, having overcome all the difficulties – snowfalls, highways covered with ice, the frontier unexpectedly closing for a night – we reached Sukhumi. It was the 31st December 2002.

We were struck by the hospitality of the locals. The people from Adzubzha cordially welcomed us and wrote letters in reply to those we had met in St Petersburg. When we returned home our bags were full of tangerines, wine and sun.

# Stewart Henderson poet and broadcaster

My limited hitch-hiking experiences are similar to my attempts at playing tennis, i.e. a lot of standing around in a bewildered way not knowing how the whole thing works. I do remember one journey from Liverpool in the early 1970s with a mate who was a bit of a 'king of the road.' Well, he'd once hitched to Colwyn Bay then got the bus back. Not exactly Jack Kerouac but it was a start.

On this occasion we were on our way to Bristol but somehow ended up in Cheddar Gorge drinking scrumpy which meant the inside of our heads felt as though they'd been pebble-dashed. On the way out of Liverpool we spent a small eternity waiting on the East Lancashire Road. As the seasons changed we eventually got a lift from a tattooed lorry driver called Neville to Stratford-upon-Avon. We spent a night near there in a barn listening to rats going about their rat business. One ran across my chest pre-empting Jennie Bond's ordeal in *I'm A Celebrity, Get Me Out Of Here*.

On the way back we were marooned in Coventry so we slept in a graveyard in the ruins of the cathedral....and neither of us became Goths. Looking back it was all very peaceful and a wonderfully carefree adventure, although sadly something I wouldn't undertake (no pun intended) now. My thumbing days are over, as is my tennis.

# Bad Trips

# Will Durst comedian

Back in the late '70s my friend Mike Haase and I sold our sandwich shop in Waukesha, Wisconsin which was called 'Crummies.' We used the 200 bucks apiece to visit his girlfriend in Minneapolis then we decided to hitch-hike to San Diego to visit a friend, so we lit out together then split up in St Louis. He went south via Highway 40 to visit a girlfriend in Flagstaff and I went west on 70 to visit a girlfriend in Colorado Springs. We determined we would meet in Vegas at the Riviera Casino. One week later we each had sixty dollars total. We kept twenty apiece and tore the third twenty in half so when we got to Vegas we would have some money left, no matter how stupid we behaved. I got stuck in Eastern Colorado and one night the three people I met in a row were all cops. One cop told me I couldn't hitch-hike on the Interstate I was on, another cop told me to get off the county trunk road I was on and the last cop woke me up the next morning under the picnic table where I was sleeping in the middle of a motel complex.

I eventually met Mike at the Riviera and when I found him he had just lost his last five bucks on red. We reattached the two torn pieces of the twenty and ate, then hitch-hiked down the strip towards Highway 15 to LA. A car passed us without his lights on and we yelled at him; he squealed to a stop, did two 180s and pulled up next to us. We leaned into the passenger window to discover a gun pointed at our heads.

"What did you say?" the driver menaced.

"Your lights. Your headlights aren't on," we stammered.

He looked down, turned them on, nodded the gun at us in acknowledgement and said, "Cool, thanks" and drove off.

We hitched a ride to LA in a bus with a cult of Manson wannabees, but that's another story altogether...

# Lembit Opik   Liberal Democrat Member of Parliament

In 1984, I was a student at Bristol University. That winter I decided to hitch-hike to Germany to raise money for charity. My fellow Bristol student, Clive Banks, came along for the ride. In order to increase our chances of getting lifts quickly, we dusted down our top hats and tails and stood at the start of the M32 looking like extras from an old Fred Astaire movie. Except that, while Mr Astaire was 'Flying Down to Rio', we felt we'd be lucky to hitch down to Reading. But the gambit worked, and within 36 hours we were freezing our nuts off in bow ties on the German border, thanks to the generous help of a chatty lorry driver called Eddie.

The return journey proved a little more 'eventful'. Arriving in icy Dover at three in the morning, a new but battered-looking Audi stopped and offered us a lift to London. Making us both sit in the back, the driver, smelling of booze and, apparently having little knowledge or regard for the UK Highway Code, held an increasingly odd and disjointed conversation with the two of us. He claimed to be a doctor, but it seemed unlikely to say the least, given his own apparent state of health, and his seeming inability to communicate effectively in any language. Clive asked if the 'doctor' was going to London on business. "No," he said, "I'm going to London to play." Realising he'd locked us in the back, we began to feel more than a little edgy about the wisdom of accepting lifts from drunk strangers at three in the morning when wearing top hats and tails.

Eventually the 'doctor' slowed the car right down, and finally stopped in the middle of nowhere in a lay-by. In the silent stand-off which followed, he made the calculation that we weren't going to London "to play," and pulled back onto the road. After some time we insisted he stop at the next service station, where we virtually had to force him to unlock the boot and get our stuff out of there. We must have looked a funny sight to the small number of people watching in the murky dawn as we, in our top hat and tails, battled with the inebriated driver in a desperate effort to unlock his boot and unload our stuff onto the frosty ground. Having retrieved our possessions, we scurried off, leaving our shifty chauffeur apparently talking to himself next to his Audi. After some time, we managed to get another lift, this time with a milkman. As we trundled along at an achingly slow pace, I thought to myself what a relief it was that this guy was driving on business, and not delivering milk 'for fun'. I thanked my lucky stars for morning deliveries 'right to your doorstep' and away from a creepy close call on the road to Rochester.

# Ralph Bakshi artist, filmmaker, writer

"When I drove it was to talk to people – to hear their thoughts, see what was going on. See what the streets brought me – who was out there. Hitch-hiking with myself – out of the studio – during Coonskin – driving to New Orleans…anywhere… This is how I came up with my movies…" – Ralph Bakshi

Just driving
LA high noon
There's no fucking air anywhere
The heat's so oppressive
The buildings stained
Brown, yellow, gray
Stucco
Cement shit
They stutter by

Rotted palm trees
Teeter shiver in haze
Can't open the windows
It's worse outside
Than the smoke-filled car

Cigarette-stained window
Shit air

All shit

I just wanted to get away from the studio
A million questions
A million lies
A million animators
Wanting me to save the industry
And all I want to do is scream
Scream at everything
Scream at everyone
Like a Soutine chicken
Twisting, turning, twisting, turning

This is the revolution
Playing panther
Playing black
Hating whites
Everyone's against something
Everyone wants something
Everyone's joining on
Dropping out
Trying to figure out
How to make a few bucks
While trying to fuck buck the system
They're employees
white on black chicks
Each other

Peter Max keeps loving everybody
Painting city buses
Not with bright colors a piece
But his name
BIG
BIG
BIG

In tall reeds
In strange settings
Twisting and screaming soldiers
Call for their brothers
Their mothers
Helicopters explode and burn
Guts mingle with daily newspapers
While peace marches spit
On the National Guard
Jane Fonda in a massive photo opportunity
Dances around North Vietnam
Calling draft dodgers
The real American heroes
And black boys

Eyes white wide
Like a bad cartoon
Watch the incoming
From every side

Wondering why
There's no more parades
That's fun

Janice dies
Hendrix dies
Morrison dies
Record executives
Ship their music
Fast
Fast
Fast
While thousands of tiers
Are still wet

*'Just Driving' © Bakshi Productions, Inc 2004*

# Lars Therkildsen historian

I remember arriving in Dresden, in the former DDR, with Rudy, a pal of mine.
At that stage I was running out of money, so while he found a hostel to sleep in,
I took my sleeping bag and found a garden to spend the night in. It was actually
too cold to sleep but I was OK when the sun started to come out in the early
morning. I woke up very abruptly after only a few hours when someone hit me
hard on the head. I opened my eyes, and there stood a little smiling kid with a
yellow plastic shovel in his hand. It turned out I had slept in a kindergarten.

Dresden was not a very pretty place. All the historic parts had been
bombed during the Second World War, so instead we continued into Germany.
My financial situation was going from bad to worse, and both of us were
getting tired of travelling. We needed to go home to wash our clothes and get
some proper food. I think it was the last ride that nearly killed us, and made
us decide to head home. We had been picked up by a young man in his late

twenties. He looked a bit thin and tired, but was otherwise very friendly. His car looked very tired too. "It's a self-built van," he explained and clapped the rusty engine hood with a tiny hand that didn't look as if it was meant to build vans. We soon found out that he not only drove the van, but also slept, ate and watched television in it. It was his home. There was a tiny bed and a tiny black and white television, and a strong smell of sour cream and onion chips everywhere. But he seemed harmless enough, so we jumped in – me in the back and Rudy in front. In the beginning things seemed O.K., but somewhere along the way Rudy turned around and whispered to me, "Hey, he's completely drunk!" I was watching some German police series on the black and white television, so I hadn't noticed that he was swallowing one beer after another and then, not very politely, throwing the empty cans out on the busy autobahn. Then suddenly he began to cry and tell us that he actually had a wife and a kid, but that she had divorced him and thrown him out of the house. This was apparently the reason why he had built the van. While keeping an eye on the road we tried to comfort him, but after a short while he began zigzagging violently, making the television set and beer cans fly all over the place. The other cars on the road were desperately honking their horns. It felt as if the car was falling apart, and it made noises like it just wanted to stop and die. Rudy and I began to fear we would join it any minute and begged him to stop the wreck and let us out. He didn't really understand any of our arguments but, luckily, in the end he did pull over and let us out. We tried to convince him to get some rest before going any further, but without listening to us he took off in his van and disappeared.

# Stephen R. Bissette  24 years in the American comic book industry
(as a cartoonist, writer, editor, publisher, and co-publisher), remains best-known for Saga of the Swamp Thing, Taboo, '1963,' Tyrant. http://www.comicon.com/bissette

### 'With My Thumb Up My...'

I've avoided hitch-hiking and hitch-hikers all my life, and so make for a rather odd riding companion in this book. I have had only three experiences of it – the sum total of my hitch-hiking experience with my fiftieth birthday mere months away – and relate this one with some trepidation, since my parents don't know about it (nor, perhaps, should they). It was, after all, their car I was driving.

I grew up in northern Vermont. While in high school (amid my first year of driving), I regularly drove Interstate 89 between Waterbury and various Burlington area exits. The constant allure for me were Burlington's movie theatres and bookstores; by the time I had my license, the Little Professor on Church Street and the Emerald City of Oz (both in Burlington) were the only places one could find underground comix, a constant draw for this budding cartoonist. On rare occasions, I would brave the drive to Montreal in search of French comics – gorgeous hard-cover collected works, unlike anything we had in America at that time – or to see a rarity like Sergio Leone's *Once Upon a Time in the West* or some odd Canadian film I'd seen commercials for (on the Canada TV stations we received). Now, this was 1972, when hitch-hiking and hitch-hikers were a key counterculture staple. I neither smoked pot nor had much hair. My friends did or had plenty of each, and regularly picked up hitch-hikers when we were out and about together. Short-haired uptight virgin non-smoking ex-Boy Scout Catholic lad that I was, I didn't. I looked like a straight-arrow for years, and acted like one for the most part, and not picking up thumb-trippers was my rule. Sure, hitching was part of the scene, and there were plenty of longhairs hitching up and down the Green Mountain State, but – well, I did pick one up. Once. And never again.

It was around 11:30 on a sunny summer morning and I was on a comix hunt. It was such a lovely day, I'd driven 'The Old Road,' Route 2, from Waterbury to Richmond, and was coming to the interstate just after leaving Richmond village. There was a fellow planted at the foot of the entrance ramp who looked about 17 – my age – with shaggy brown hair, scant beard, worn denim pants and jacket, back pack, and his thumb out. He looked like a regular enough guy; he was turning to look at the car that had just passed him by. He didn't display the kind of body language you sometimes saw from a hitcher who'd just been passed by – no sagging of the shoulders, no dropping of the head, and no flash of the finger at the ass end of the car. Nothing in his demeanour suggested any disappointment. He just kept his thumb out and turned to watch them pass. He had his backpack in the other hand; with it off his back I could see a fairly decent version of Mr. Natural hand-painted on the back of his denim jacket, and I reckon that clinched it: I mean, here I was hoping to find some new comix in the big city, and here's Robert Crumb's comix guru on the road, so to speak. Besides, I thought, Burlington is just a couple exits up the road – that must be where this guy was headed, right? University of Vermont, probably. No sweat. So I pulled over and picked up this guy, who happily jumped into my passenger seat with "Thanks, I'm Mike," and off we went.

He was a little nervous, but so was I. I'd turned the radio down when he got in and kept it that way, it seems, for the duration. I wanted to compliment him on the Mr. Natural on his jacket, maybe get a better look at it, but that seemed stupid, so I just stuck to basics.

I asked where he was going, and he flashed a smile and said, "Oh, just a couple exits up," and I told him where I was going, and he stopped smiling and then said, "Great, that's good," and shut up for a bit.

Though it was a hot day and he sported a marijuana leaf image on his T-shirt, he didn't smell of either sweat or pot, but a bead of sweat did run down by his ear after he stopped talking. He fumbled around in his backpack for a minute, then put it down by his feet.

The radio was still low, the music unrecognizable and muted. "Hey, I've got a great tape we could play on the way," he finally said, rather flatly.

"Uh, sorry, no tape-player in this car," I replied; it was true.

Still, he said, "But I've got it right here..." and then trailed off. He fumbled around in his pack a bit; only in hindsight did his moving his right arm down to the edge of his seat before letting his pack slide back to the floor harbour anything of significance. He turned and looked out his window, and seemed a little furtive. Nothing unusual. I mean, he didn't know me from Adam, I didn't know him, and the artificial intimacy of the car's front seat began to seem a bit imposing, but what the hell, we were just on our way to Burlington, right? We were just passing Taft's Corners, an essentially vacant four-corner junction on Route 2 visible to the right off 89, with a run-down little store there. A landmark, though; the Shelburne exit was coming up soon.

"So, where do you want to get off in Burlington?" I said as evenly as I could. "I'll be heading for Church Street, so I can go by way of Shelburne Road or get off by Gayne's and go up by the dorms..."

He didn't reply, just kept looking out his window, then cleared his throat a little. "Well, OK, huh, Church Street..." He trailed off again, then stole a glance over to me. He was beginning to seem really nervous. "I was kinda hoping to go up a bit further."

Ever-agreeable, I said, "Well, OK, I can get off at Winooski, cross over the bridge, and drive up toward the campus that way –"

He cleared his throat sharply, cutting me off. "No, that won't do it," he whispered, and stole another sharp glance at me. "I've got to go a bit further."

Well, this sucked, didn't it? At this point, I wasn't worried, but I was beginning to get a little ticked. I mean, I had said where I was headed and all. -

My passenger shifted in his seat, keeping his eyes ahead, and said it again: "I've got to go a bit further up." A beat. The radio, still muffled, kept droning. God, it was nice outside. "I mean, really, I do. I mean, I've got to get to Montreal."

Now I was nervous. What the fuck? MONTREAL? I think I stammered, "Uh, but, I'm not going to Montreal."

"No sweat, I'll let you out at the exit further north, then," I recovered. "You'll be a lot closer than you were –"

"You're not hearing me," he said, "I've got to get to Montreal." He looked over to me, dead serious, his hair hanging in his eyes a bit, more sweat dripping down by his ear. "I've really got to get to Montreal, like, today... Now."

Now, Montreal was a bit of a haul, way past my game plan. Besides, that's not how this was supposed to work; I mean, I'd been with my friends when they'd picked up hitch-hikers, and it seemed to be the rule of the road as far as I could tell that you went where you were going, and unless they were headed in that direction, the ride was refused – or ended at the nearest exit that would get them further along.

"I've got a joint I can offer," he said with the same flat voice. "It's pretty decent, if you can take me – "

"Thanks, sorry," I replied, "I don't smoke, but thanks. OK, look, I'll let you off at Winooski –"

"You're not hearing me," he replied, neither raising nor lowering his voice, but sounding a bit of a threat now. My mouth was dry, chalk-dry, and now I didn't want to look at my passenger. I especially didn't want to look when something glinted by his leg – metal – and without a word he tipped the blade of a medium-sized hunting knife up into view and, with a casual tip of his right hand, lay the blade down flat atop his right knee, pointing away from his door. To me. I looked at that blade, then into my rear-view mirror, then out to the road, then back to the mirror, then back to the blade, and finally back to him. He wasn't looking at me; he was looking away, out his window.

I tried to say something, and choked on whatever it was.

He looked back at me, and said, "Montreal?" I nodded, unable to say anything. "Yes?" he said, still no change in tenor or tone, and I nodded again, breaking a sweat.

And with that, the blade was gone, he was reaching back down into his backpack, and the radio droned on, and I don't recall saying another word until I was asked where I lived. But it took a while – between a half hour and forty-five minutes – to get to that.

In fact, I don't recall any details of the trip; everything that led from the Richmond entrance ramp to the revelation of the knife and the implicit threat is vivid in my memory. The rest is a blur; not so much forgotten as denied at the time of the occurrence. A long, interminable blur – only the duration seems real – *sans* any detail to speak of. No cops were visible along the road at any point; countless cars, trucks, and tractor-trailers whizzed by, but what could I do? The only salvation seemed to be in getting him to Montreal. I could do that, couldn't I? It wasn't that much further to go. Well, an hour and a half or so. A ways. But I could make it, couldn't I?

Nothing more happened, really. I drove him to Montreal. That's it. It's a blur, I suspect, because it was so uneventful; the event — the glimpse of that blade, the threat – had already passed. All that was left to do was endure the trek. I recall looking somewhat wistfully at the St. Albans Drive-In screen, visible to the west from 89 after we passed the St. Albans exit, and hoping I would be able to see a movie there again: one of the few concessions my mind made to the worst happening. Like, what if I didn't survive this ride? What if he pulls that knife out again? What if he uses it? He wouldn't, would he? What was I thinking when I picked him up?

Oh, ya. Mr. Natural. He had Mr. Natural on his jacket. Be cool, Flakey Foont. Flakey picks up a hitch-hiker. Zen lesson. Hope this stays a Mr. Natural comic and doesn't become Thrilling Murder Comix; Crumb's psycho Manson caricature came to mind, fucking and killing. Don't go there. Montreal. Go to Montreal instead. Just get to Montreal.

There was customs to deal with – by my experience, Canada was easy to get into, but the return trip (especially for a teenager) often involved the car being searched and stern looks with stern questions. But that would be coming back — going up was usually a piece of cake, but it still made me nervous, the scrutiny and questions and all. Like I said, uptight virgin ex-Boy Scout lapsed Catholic boy and all, I always felt guilty.

"Where do you live?" the customs agent asked me, and that's the next thing I remember vividly.

I just said, "Colbyville, Vermont," and I reflexively added, "by Waterbury," as I always did, because nobody knew where Colbyville was, and the agent looked from me to my passenger, and asked the same, and I heard the name of some town and then, "Connecticut," and the agent asked where we were going, and my passenger said "Montreal," and was it business or pleasure, and we both said "pleasure," at the same time, which was a lucky thing, and the agent looked me in the eye, and asked how long we'd be there, and I said "just today," and I almost said, "Jesus Christ, I'm coming back as soon as I can," but didn't, which was also a good thing, and I think he asked if we were carrying anything into Canada with us, and I said "no" and then the customs guy waved us on, and we somehow got through, though I was playing all kinds of whacked scenarios of what I shoulda said, shoulda done, and my passenger just said, "Cool," and said to me, "Stay cool, it's OK, I just need to be in Montreal, please just get me there, I'm not going to do anything, just get me to Montreal, OK, please?" and we kept driving, and I thought, "He just said please?," and it was fine, it was OK now, but it sucked, it sucked sooooo bad, and I was so scared.

We drove that seemingly endless stretch through rural Quebec, where the land goes dead flat, peppered with just a few houses and farms and farm stands and French signs and vast expanses of corn. The radio was a low hiss by now, long out-of-distance of WDEV, the Waterbury radio station, and at some point my passenger reached over and turned it off, and hummed to himself, off and on, and said something to me, but nothing registered until he said, "up here, you stay straight," and he began to occasionally give directions, "up here, you've got to get on 10," and I listened and followed every one of 'em and the road got wider and traffic heavier and the corn was gone and there were more billboards than I'd ever seen (they're illegal in Vermont, natch) and we somehow got into Montreal without my making a single wrong turn or error and somehow there we were in the hubbub and he said "I'll get off here," just as we got into the city proper, and I pulled over and almost hit the curb and stopped short and he opened the door and he actually said, "Thanks, really."

I don't recall him getting out, but I do remember the backpack – with the knife inside – being lifted off the floor, and drifting out the door, and that was when I knew I was OK and it was alright and I'd get home just fine. He leaned back in, and my heart thumped in my chest, and I looked over, and he looked at me one more time and said, "No, really, thanks, and sorry, I mean, really, I had to get here now, I – " and, "Uh, OK, well, bye," he was gone, and the door shut, and Mr. Natural waved before the backpack was slung up and over his face and beard and nose and robe and seeing it again for a moment, it didn't really look like such a good copy of Crumb after all – why did I stop and pick this guy up? – and Mr. Natural was gone and the backpack shifted into place and hitch-hike guy was walking away, up the street, and I began to shake, and almost hit a truck pulling away from the curb, and somehow found my way around a few blocks and out the fuck of Montreal.

I got lost twice before the straight, steady shot back to Vermont. I pulled over twice, once to puke my guts out and once 'cuz I couldn't stop shaking. I was shaking the way one of my father's heating-oil-delivery drivers used to when he was needing a bottle: spastic shakes that started mid-spine and shook me to the core, coming in waves I couldn't stem. I've only felt them one other time in my life (when a Port Authority cop wouldn't let me board my bus and left me stranded in New York City without a dime), and I thought they'd never stop. By the time I got back to the border, I'd calmed down enough to make it through customs – didn't even get searched – and then I was driving into Vermont, blessed green Vermont, and when I saw the St. Albans Drive-In screen again I almost cried, and started to shake again, and pulled over one last time and just sat by the side of the highway until I realized I was hungry and thirsty. And safe.

When I came up over the crest of the highway by the Sunset Drive-In in Winooski, I remembered the radio and turned it on again. I even went to the Little Professor and picked up a couple of comix (no Mr. Natural).

I didn't tell anyone what had happened; I didn't want to lose car privileges, and knew if I told one of my friends word would get back to my parents. So I buttoned my lip and said nothing. I avoided trips north for a couple of weeks, but that soon passed; simply put, there was nothing to do in Montpelier, and the action was in Burlington. I went to Montreal later that fall on my own, just to get over that hump; to go there and get back without trauma, just to do it. But I never picked up another hitch-hiker in my fucking life unless it was somebody I knew, and that's that.

I've passed the same advice on to my two kids, and never hitch-hike myself – save one time.

I have, in fact, walked over ten miles of country road in pitch-dark night between midnight and 3 am rather than hitch. The closest friends of my first wife Marlene and I were having their second baby, and Marlene had gone on ahead; I had a deadline comic art job to finish, and took the bus to Waterbury long after she'd arrived at our friends' home in Stowe. The baby hadn't arrived yet, but our pregnant friend was in labour; with that news fresh in my ear, I took the bus ride north, with the arrangement that they'd pick me up at the bus stop in Waterbury once I got there.

All I had to do was call.

I got off the bus in Waterbury around 11:30 pm, found the pay phone across the street from what used to be Vincent's Pharmacy, and called and called and called.

No answer at our friends' house. Worrying that something had gone wrong, that everyone was at the hospital, and without enough money in my pocket to pay for a cab ride (if there was a cab to find – this was, after all, the sleepy little burg of Waterbury), I decided the only thing for me to do was walk the ten miles or so from Waterbury to Stowe.

So I made my way to Route 100. It was a long walk, and after I cleared Colbyville and the last street light, it was a long DARK walk. At one point, I stepped in something furry and soft: road kill. My sneaker now wet with whatever, I grimaced and scraped my sneaker as best I could on the tarmac. I don't know what I'd stepped in, but was grateful it wasn't a porcupine carcass. I almost stepped off the shoulder once or twice; I was dog-tired, and worried about my friends.

What happened? Where were they? Something must have gone terribly wrong – was the baby OK? Was the mother OK? Fearing the worst, I walked to and through Waterbury Center, stopping at the only pay phone I knew of in town and called Stowe again – still no answer. I went back to walking; I was halfway there, just about.

As I was coming out of the village proper a sleek little sportscar veered past me, swerved, and pulled over. I was offered a ride, but I declined. The blonde woman in the passenger seat insisted, and insisted, so I shrugged and agreed to get in, which I immediately regretted. As the woman tipped her seat forward to let me into the back, I could smell liquor. The guy in his forties driving was soused. So was she. Jesus, they were drunk – roaring drunk. They were also arguing, but they sure wanted company, and lucky me, I was it. I was repeatedly offered drinks, but declined, and realized that I'd definitely blown it getting into this car. While knocking back another nip, the driver almost clocked a mailbox, and they both laughed, and I planned my exit strategy; there was a house up ahead I remembered, and we were almost there. Stowe was still a ways away, but after they nearly collided with a second truck, I lied and said, "Oh, this is where I'm going, right up here on the right." They pulled over, almost slipping into the ditch before the driveway, and I got out.

They laughed and said, "Glad to have been able to help!" I got out, waved, and pretended to walk up the driveway of the house we'd stopped in front of. They tore off the shoulder and buzzed toward Stowe. When they were out of sight, I got back on Route 100 and walked another five miles without a hitch (pun intended).

(Just to provide a proper finale, I will tell you that I wandered into Stowe that night and tried the first pay phone I came to. Still no answer. I walked the couple of miles through Stowe and out the other end, eventually reaching my friends' home. There was our car in our driveway, which Marlene had driven up the day before; there was our friends' car. I knocked on the door, then a window, and my bleary-eyed friend opened the door. Turned out the baby was born the night before – a girl – mom and daughter were well.

"Why didn't you call?" my friend blurted out, half-awake. After insisting I had, time and time again, he admitted sheepishly they'd forgotten about the plans we'd made, and it turned out they had unplugged the phones because everyone was exhausted.

(Ya, tell me about it.)

Keep your thumbs in your pocket, and happy trails.

## Larry Tucker  management consultant
### 'Hijacking for Medicinal Purposes – 1974'

I'd been hitching for three months and ended up broke in the Hague and trying to get home. A couple of Dutch friends finally bought me a ferry ticket for the next morning and I hitched to the Hoek van Holland and got the boat.

When I got to Harwich I began to feel really sick – stomach ache and a kind of fever building up. I had to get home and I knew the road was never very good so it would be a long haul. I started hitching and, before too long, a middle-aged bloke stopped and I jumped in. I only had a small kitbag, and I pushed it over into the back seat.

He seemed OK at first: "Where have you been, what did you do? Ooh, all them girls!" The usual.

Anyway, in those days (I was seventeen) I had long blond hair which curled very prettily I guess (even when filthy) and I had had my fair share of propositions from blokes, especially in the Arab countries (and a few from women!) but I didn't used to take any shit from those guys that became pushy. It was bad because I was ill and this guy put his hand on my leg and was saying what he'd like to do.

Well, without seeming uncooperative, I asked him to stop the car while I took a leak. As I got out I puked up and I knew then I couldn't give up this lift, and I knew my kitbag was in the back. So I climbed in the back of the car, pulled out my knife and held it to the back of his neck and said drive. He began to cry. I felt bad, but powerful, and he started explaining some medical problem he had with his dick or something, which meant he couldn't have sex. I began to apologise but I knew I had to have this lift. I got him to drive me over one hundred miles away, we even stopped for petrol! But when he dropped me I was so feverish, I think he realised that he could have pushed me over with a feather. But too late, I was gone.

I spent the night on the central reservation of a dual carriageway, delirious and dry retching, hallucinating gargoyles in the car headlights as they flashed through the grass. In the morning I hitched south and got lifts I don't even remember, but I made it home and recovered to wonder what the hell I'd done.

## Sir Alan Parker film director/writer

It was outside a youth hostel in Paris that I encountered my worst hitch-hiking experience. No sooner had my friend Brian Stacey and I walked out of the building when a greasy, sweaty bloke pulled up his Peugeot 203 with the offer of a lift. The back seat was full of old car parts so Brian and I squeezed into the front seat.

Five minutes into the lift, the driver started rubbing his genitals and produced a bundle of pornographic pictures from the glove compartment. We smiled politely for a bit, but when he made a grab for poor Brian Stacey's thigh we both yanked at the handbrake and clambered out.

Curious that this memory has stayed with me – weird that I even remember the car – and I have no interest in cars. It's the very reason, I suppose, why hitch-hiking gradually lost its allure. Such an innocent pursuit: cheap travel in a more generous age suddenly became more hazardous when the crazies started to exploit it.

# Rhodri Morgan First Minister of the Welsh Assembly

Some of your hitch-hiking experiences bring your life into such sharp focus that even forty years later you can remember the details quite graphically as though they had taken place last weekend.

Some forty years ago when I was a student in the USA I did spend part of my summer vacation hitch-hiking in the Appalachian Mountains. I thought that as this was coal-mining territory where a lot of Welsh emigrated a hundred years previously, I would see a lot of similarities physically in the 'feel' of the communities. The first supposition was right but I am not sure the second was. Certainly, the hills of West Virginia do look like the South Wales coalfield plateau, with deeply incised valleys and the slag heaps and trains full of coal wagons.

However, the communities just don't feel the same at all. There is a feeling of impermanence about the mining communities in the USA that has never struck me about the Welsh coalfield valleys. I remember being picked up by two young men, one of them perhaps still in late high school, eighteen or so, and the other in his mid-twenties, a shade older than me, called Billy, with floppy blond locks that might, with luck, have got him to Hollywood and out of the very depressed mining communities. He wanted, after talking to me and picking up on my British accent, to take me back to his home because he had married an English woman from around Oxford while in the Air Force. He was very excited when I said that was where I had just finished at university. He said his wife never had the chance to meet anybody from Oxford and felt very 'lonesome' etc.

The houses were all of this slightly impermanent character, although well stocked and with lots of fridges and accoutrements, and with bags of Government welfare foodstuffs stacked everywhere you looked – flour, sugar, potatoes, etcetera – all clearly stamped 'food stamps programme', something which had disappeared from our welfare programmes back at the end of World War II.

He introduced me to his wife. She was very quiet rather than sullen or unhappy. She was very much an Oxford townie with a strong 'burr' in her accent and obviously none too happy this far away from home. She carried on cooking. We all had a meal together and a few beers and then later on, while I was talking away to his wife at about half past nine, some sixth sense or instinct took over. I just suddenly clocked that Billy wasn't there any longer and, swinging my eyes over to the little refrigerator which was next to the back door where we had come in, I noticed that the pistol casually placed on top of the fridge, which I had noticed on coming in, was gone.

I suddenly turned to Billy's wife and said, "Billy's not here and I notice the pistol has gone."

She replied, "Yes, he likes to go out driving the car round the hills this time of night when he has had a few beers and he always takes his revolver with him."

Showing a surprising degree of decisiveness for a chattering class graduate student, I carried on: "Is that pistol loaded?"

"Always."

"OK," I said. "He's had quite a few beers. When he comes back is he likely to suddenly accuse you and me of getting up to something we shouldn't be?"

"Yes, that is quite possible. He is quite like that when he has had a few drinks. He goes out at night with the gun and drives the car as fast as he can round and round all the mountain tracks round here, but you never know what he might do when he gets back."

"Well, I want to get out of here now," I said. "Is there anywhere else that I can go?" This was not the kind of mining settlement with any hotels or guest houses.

"I'll take you down to Billy's mother's house and you will be OK there," she said.

No sooner said than done. She led me out of the back of the house down some alleyways, up lots of stairs and down lots of fire escapes and we soon arrived at Billy's mother's house. There was a hushed conversation between Billy's wife and her mother-in-law and I was led into a cellar-like bedroom where I very gratefully got into bed. It had the dampest feel of any bed that I have ever climbed into or slept in, but never was I so grateful to slip between the sheets.

In the morning I went back up to Billy's house for breakfast. Nothing said. Nothing mentioned. The pistol was back on top of the small kitchen fridge next to the back door. All the empty beer cans safely stowed in the kitchen waste bin. I set off to see another day hitch-hiking but the memory still stays fresh with me after forty years. Sometimes you have to stop talking the talk and you have to walk the walk.

# Christopher Sykes H.M. Diplomatic Service
### 'Taiwan 1981 – Cross Island Highway'

I was with my wife bussing and hitching around the island trying to get from Tai Choy on the west coast, by crossing the middle of the country to Hua Liam on the eastern side. This required several methods to get through some treacherous roads through the mountains.

We had reached a mountain village called, I think, Pu Xi, on a bus made for about thirty people. We counted over a hundred getting off. We managed to hitch a lift then towards the next village with a local businessman, but a few miles further on, we came to an abrupt halt at a huge landslide which had taken away much of the road.

Earthquake tremors were not uncommon in this area, so these may have been the cause. We decided to climb over the obstruction and clambered down over the other side to rejoin the road. Having then walked a few hundred yards we came to a junction. Minutes later, an open utility vehicle with two workers in the cab came by. We stuck out our thumbs and it immediately stopped. I explained about the landslide and, eager to help, he told us to get in the back. I should add that Westerners, especially in the mountains, were a rare sight, so we had a certain novelty value, I suppose.

As we went round sharp bends at speed we became quite frightened. The long back of the open truck swung out over the edge of the road which, more often than not, was the start of a precipitous drop of over six or seven hundred feet to the bottom of the Taroko Gorge. From time to time, we caught glimpses of objects, sometimes shattered vehicles or other equipment on the hillside below us, evidence of previous errors of judgement.

At last we reached the next town – the workers' destination. As we bade them farewell, I noticed the familiar glazed look in the driver's eyes and the red stain on his lips telling us he had been chewing a local beetlenut – the mild hallucinogenic commonly used by the hill people. We surmised it was probably to stave off the fear of driving on those terrible roads – or perhaps just because it made it more fun. For them, that is.

# Cosey Fanni Tutti multimedia artist

I hitch-hiked a lot when I was young, in fact I started hitch-hiking when I was under 10 years old. My friend Lelli and I used to thumb lifts to the seaside during the school summer holidays. We'd sit together in the back giggling as we made farting noises on our arms and blaming each other for it. Typical kids' stuff really, which must have a been a pain in the neck for the driver.

We stopped when we failed to get a lift home one night and we had to catch the bus giving our names and addresses because we had no money. I got a thrashing from my father, and was kept in for a month with no pocket money and forbidden to see Lelli. It was around the time of the Moors Murders so my father was white with fear that something had happened to me. His relief at my safety was to hurt me (?) Mad.

After I left home at 17 and lived with Gen we hitch-hiked everywhere. We only lived on about £3 a week then – crazy as it sounds – so we never even thought of catching a bus or train to where we were going and neither of us could drive. So me, Gen and our dog Tremble would travel the UK visiting friends and family. We were unconventional dressers to say the least, so it was always a bit of a struggle to get a lift. We took to a strategy of Gen hiding in the bushes behind me while I stood on the roadside hitching a lift with Tremble. Then when a car stopped, me, Tremble and Gen would get in the car, much to the astonishment of the driver.

I guess we took advantage of male drivers wanting to help a vulnerable woman and her bedraggled dog. Of course we were also aware that they may have had ulterior motives but we were quite aggressive in our youth and consequently fearless.

I remember there was a kind of hitch-hiking etiquette – that as payment for your lift you'd talk with the driver and keep them company. In all my time hitch-hiking I've never ever got a lift from a woman driver. Quite understandable, I suppose. Plus if I think about it being the late '60s/early '70s there wasn't the proliferation of women drivers on long journeys that you have today. Funny how you take so much for granted.

One thing that sticks in my mind is that there'd be a cluster of hitchers at the Tinsley turn off, which was like the gateway to London and beyond for people hitching from the North. It was a very competitive spot but there was a kind of unwritten code that whoever got there first got the first lift and so on. But then you had to accept the reality that a driver who stops chooses who they want in their car.

My most vivid memory of hitch-hiking is being cold, wet and tired. A feeling of abandonment which immediately changes into elation and triumph when you get a lift.

From all the lifts from strangers I never once had a bad experience – boring maybe, but not threatening. The only time I was in danger was when I hitched alone and a 'friend' stopped and gave me a lift. That was my first experience of attempted rape. Thankfully he backed off when I got violent and he drove me home. I haven't hitch-hiked since.

# Irv Thomas veteran hitch-hiker, author of *Derelict Days... Sixty Years on the Roadside Path to Enlightenment*

## 'An Incident on the Autobahn'

My hitch-hiking days as a youngster in the 1940s had come to seem the very symbol of youthful innocence in a middle age plagued by the hassles of trying to get ahead in a resistant world. So it was only natural that I would regard it as the prime avenue of my eventual attempt to reclaim that lost sense of innocence.

I returned to hitch-hiking when I was 44, and made it the centrepiece of a re-dedicated life. Not to the pursuit of innocence *per se*, but to a reconsidered spectrum of what makes life worthwhile: a de-emphasis of material values in favour of the spiritual, the creative, and the unchained expression of personal freedom. This new life ultimately took me on a free-roving exploration of Britain and Europe, detailed in a book entitled *Innocence Abroad: Adventuring through Europe at 64 on $100 per week*. And I am pleased to present a short piece from that book as a testimonial in this one – a testimonial to hitch-hiking as the handmaiden of Providence. For I regard the insight of a true and existent Providence at work in our lives as one of the finest gifts that hitch-hiking offers.

By its very aspect, you see, of putting us in the hands of chance, hitch-hiking provides proof, time and time again, that we live in a provident universe. But sometimes, as in this tale you are about to read, we receive such a resounding demonstration of it as to extinguish any remaining vestige of doubt.

This story took place on a heavily travelled autobahn in Germany, outside of Nürnberg, in the summer of 1991. I had spent the prior night in the sheltering apartment of a host named Klaus, from the Servas network of folks here and there who willingly offer hospitality to travellers like me.

Over a send-off breakfast on Monday morning, Klaus told me of the Wanderjahre tradition: the wandering year of a young apprentice who has learned his art and goes out to share his skills among the people he meets along the way, for sustenance and shelter. He can go anywhere during his wander, but cannot return home until the year is done. I thought about the circumstance that my own year abroad would reach fullness in just a little more than a month. But what had been my apprenticeship . . . the rarefied art of living in innocence? Had I really become a journeyman at it?

Klaus cleared the dishes away and then took me in his zippy yellow roadster for what seemed a long ride out on the highway toward Munich, finally arriving at a busy service stop on the autobahn, the perfect place from which to resume my Wanderjahre. It was an unusually bright morning and I felt singularly alive and high as I walked to the far end of the service area, picked my spot and unhitched the pack on my back to set myself for another go at the road – when a sudden momentary catch between my chest and throat alerted me to something all too familiar; but I was too busy untangling myself from the pack to make the instant response it called for.

In those few seconds of delay, I blew it. A tachycardia attack had taken hold. My heart was speeding off like Klaus' yellow roadster, in a race with itself, and I had lost the moment to apply the brakes.

I can't recall how long I've been dealing with tachycardia. I do remember some scary times it has put me through, going back at least twenty years. It takes over the body with a sudden flush and weakness, and one can barely keep going at minimal energy level. It might take a half-hour or the whole day to run its course – I've never had the fear-free patience to wait and see. I work at stopping it, for there is no other choice. It takes the spine out of one's being, and the mind can dwell on nothing else while it's happening.

Over the years, I've learned a few methods for snapping the heartbeat back to normal, but like a bacterium that develops a drug-resistant strain each has run its course of effectiveness and no longer works for me. The only consistently reliable counter-measure has been a response in the first few moments of fluttering pulse: stop everything and breathe deliberately and deeply, holding the first lung-full of air for a moment and then slowly and evenly letting it out all the way, doing a mental count at the proper rhythm. But the deep and slow breathing must begin immediately, before the tachycardia gains a momentum that is far more difficult to break.

The moment I realized it had gotten away from me I knew I was in trouble. With traffic pounding all around me, people looking at me from every direction (the idiotic things we worry about!), nowhere to hide, no place to go for help — as if I even knew what help to seek, miles out on the autobahn from Nürnberg . . . What to do?

In dizziness and uncertainty, free of panic only because I hadn't the energy for it, I sat down cross-legged beside the onrushing traffic, put my earplugs in place and tried to find the calm for a return to deep breathing. But it was impossible, trapped between that maelstrom out there and the one going on inside my head.

I looked desperately around for a way out of the maddening highway situation. A restaurant stood nearby, but the last thing I wanted was a social setting that required any effort at normalcy. I wanted to be alone somewhere. I saw a path to the side of the restaurant going through the trees, and I followed it — into a sheltered, rustic garden area curiously graced with a small stone Celtic cross, and no one in sight. A narrow bench faced the cross, a seating for one, as if it had been ordered for the very moment. I sat down to figure out what next in this situation of no options.

I tried again to meditate there, but it just wasn't happening. I tried one of the tricks I learned years ago when an attack had once driven me to a Berkeley emergency ward: holding a deep breath as tightly as possible while trying at the same time, with all available force, to exhale it. It had worked for me then and maybe once or twice since. But it only resulted now in profuse sweating.

I considered getting someone to call for medical assistance . . . but that brought a whole other range of problems into prospect. No insurance, for one thing, and I was not quite ready to trade off my shallow funds for the riddance of my shallow heartbeat. Every avenue seemed hopeless. Must I get out on the road in this condition and try for a ride? How would I even handle it if I got one?

I'd once read a believable interview with a woman who led a hitch-hiking life, who said she'd continue to thumb when she became ill, and a doctor would pick her up. It sounds far-fetched, I know, but one rule of innocence is that the answer to any serious problem is to be found somewhere in one's immediate world. And it had always worked that way for me. I could hardly fault it even now, for this secluded glen at least gave me a measure of peace — however small the consolation. But what else was here for me?

After maybe an hour of this debilitated agonizing – which might have been a form of prayer, sitting there in front of a mystic cross, though I had no such conscious intent – a strange idea popped into my head. I recalled how medical attendants, in the case of a suddenly failed heart, would beat on a victim's chest . . . massively, with solid blows. Ready to try anything, I fisted my right hand and hit my chest over the heart as solidly as I could.

Nothing changed.

But I had pulled my punch, I thought. It's not easy to pound yourself that way with full abandon. I closed my eyes, tried to release myself to a total effort and did it again. Still nothing.

Once more, and a roundhouse swing, doing my damnedest this time to forget it was my own body I was slamming . . .

I rammed myself so hard that for a dazed moment I thought something was different . . . but it was different – I was breathing easily. I quickly grabbed a wrist to check my pulse and felt it steady and strong. The tachycardia was gone!

I sat there in an indescribable moment of relief, hardly daring to move lest it undo the results of that marvellous inspiration. I shall probably never know where it came from, whether out of left brain or right. Nor how I knew enough to keep trying until that successful third slam.

Back on the highway again, my spirits soared as only on a spring day. It felt like I'd been let free after standing on a gallows, or magically become a stripling despite my sixty-four years. It put me into a carefree, singing space, and when another hitch-hiker turned up not more than a few minutes later, a tall and gangly young fellow dressed in short pants and tank top with a big floppy-brim hat, I was quickly into conversation with him. From Hamburg, way to the north, and heading for Innsbruck, Austria, he spoke English easily and was a good deal curious as to how I found the hitching "at your age." (Ha! ... If he but knew.) The implication, of course, was that drivers would hardly be stopping for an old man. And even as I pointed out, in reply, that all kinds of people sit behind the wheel, one actually – then and there – pulled over for me.

For the two of us, as it turned out. A middle-aged fellow going to Munich, and he spoke only German; but the gods, now working smoothly for me, had provided a translator in my sudden roadside friend. I saw to it that he took the front seat, while I sat in the rear. It wasn't long before we stopped so they could switch places up front – our driver apparently weary at the wheel from a long morning on the road. I silently gave it my blessing (for wasn't I now precisely at the centre of Grace?)

## Jenny Jones an active campaigner for environmental and social justice since 1970, and an elected Green Party Member of the London Assembly
**www.greenparty.org.uk**

As a teenager in the sixties I hitch-hiked a lot, in England and abroad, and absolutely always with a friend. It was usually my school friend Hilary. We would take it in turns to sit in the back, to sleep or read, while the front seat person had the duty of keeping the driver awake, and chatting. It was so easy to hitch-hike then, and seemed quite safe, so I have some wonderful memories of the interesting and kind people we met, but there are also a few bad memories.

In the spring of 1968, Hilary and I hitch-hiked, as we often did, from our home town Brighton to London, where we were both students. We were picked up by a normal-looking, friendly-faced man in a rather comfortable car. It was my turn in the front passenger seat, and I tried to make conversation with the driver, but it was difficult. We were barrelling along quite fast, probably exceeding the speed limit, when, to our astonishment, the driver began mumbling, then fumbling with his clothes, and we realised he had began to masturbate. My first reaction was to shout at him, but it was over even before I could get over the shock and get the words out. I just asked Hilary for a tissue for him, then told him to stop and let us out.

The incident didn't put either of us off hitch-hiking, but the phrase, "Have you got a tissue?" was a sure-fire way of getting a round of hysterical laughter.

# Marc Schmolz haulier

### 'France-Germany 1970'

The reason why I didn't initially go hitch-hiking was because of all the scares surrounding it at the time. But then my mate who had just left the army fancied going to the South of France. So he said to me "Let's go together, let's hitch-hike." He was an experienced bloke, a lieutenant in the army so I thought that I could trust him and that he could look after himself. So we started hitch-hiking from Germany and in no time – six or seven hours or so – we came to the French border at Mulhouse, just below Strasbourg.

From then on it was just a nightmare. We were standing for hours and hours, occasionally getting lifts for a couple of miles. We ended up one evening at a little village in a pub where there were lots of people playing chess. My mate was pretty good at chess and spoke a bit of French too. He told me to wait outside to try and hitch a lift while he played chess with the locals for drinks. After ten or fifteen minutes he came out with glasses of wine, beer, Pernod – the lot. And we got really, really drunk but I was still standing there trying to get a lift. I got so fed up with it in the end I just lay across the road. The traffic didn't stop, it just drove round me. I was sitting down in these flared jeans and got so frustrated that I started ripping them in anger. I ripped them right up to my knee. Ten or fifteen strips hung from my knee downwards.

Eventually a tractor came along and picked us up and carried us to the nearest town. On the way there we met another hitch-hiker, a nice French guy and he said we had no problems staying overnight as he knew the vicar in the local church. We slept there. When we woke up in the morning he was gone and all our money had gone. We had only the money in our pockets. I think he was doing this quite regularly, going backwards and forwards, pretending to be a nice guy, telling these stories, you know. We stayed for about four days and then had enough money to get the train back to Mulhouse. Then we crossed the border and started hitching again. There was an American soldier who was heading north to Hamburg and we said we wanted to go to Dortmund, which is sort of halfway. He took us. After spending many hours driving up to Dortmund we became friends and he took us home, where my Granny made a good old dinner. The soldier stayed the night and then left for Hamburg.

The funny side of it is that I never wanted to hitch-hike in the first place. When we started off we got a lift in five minutes and I thought that

was brilliant. We got all the way down to southern Germany and into France. Then in France we waited for hours and didn't get lifts. That was my first attempt at hitch-hiking and my last attempt at hitch-hiking.

## Rick Wakeman keyboard musician with group Yes and TV 'raconteur'

I actually was never a hitch-hiker myself, except for just the one occasion. My friend Trevor Alvey and myself were having a lads' holiday in Portsmouth. We were 16 years old. Whilst down there we used to go to the funfair a lot 'chasing girls', if I remember correctly. (I can't think why on earth we would go there otherwise!) Anyway, we met two girls towards the end of the holiday who lived in Basingstoke and we decided, at the end of the tour, to surprise them and go and see them. The problem was we only had enough money to buy the train ticket to Basingstoke, so we thought we would get there and worry about how to get to London after that.

We eventually arrived in Basingstoke, found the address where the two girls (sisters) lived and knocked on their door. An upstairs window opened and the two girls stuck their heads out and said just two words to us, the second being "off", if I remember rightly.

With no money, there was only one method of getting back to London and that was hitch-hiking. After four hours getting soaked by the roadside, a Hillman Minx convertible pulled up. We clambered in but, even with the roof on, the water bucketed in. We eventually arrived at Heathrow where he dropped us off and I reverse-charged a telephone call to my dad who came out and picked us up.

I never hitch-hiked again and only picked up one myself. The man concerned complained bitterly about my car, wanted me to stop and buy him something to drink and to give him money. That was the first and last time as far as I was concerned.

## Peter Lashleigh lecturer
### 'Entente Cordiale – Ste Mère-Eglise 1972'

I was hitching on my own towards St Malo on a B road where a truck had dropped me an hour or so earlier. I had placed my rucksack strategically facing the oncoming traffic, its Union Jack sewn onto the side for all to see. At that time it was generally felt that one needed to identify oneself due to bad feeling against many hitch-hikers, mostly Americans and Germans. Apparently the French were well disposed towards the English.

A Renault 17TS (I later owned one and had always liked them), sped towards me and passed without slowing. Suddenly the brakes went on, it shuddered to a halt and reversed at speed, front wheels spinning, towards me. The driver's electric window slid down and an unshaven, manic face began to hurl abuse at me. He spat at me with commendable power, then turned to the passenger seat. He produced a sawn-off shotgun which he cocked as he leaned it on his left arm. I dived into the nearest hedgerow, terrified. He laughed and called me something about the rear end of an English cow, then sped off, tyres spinning in a cloud of dust. Having recovered myself I got to the nearest café and drank about four Ricards. In between glasses, I removed the Union Jack.

# Jim W. MacKenzie heating engineer
## 'Dissident in Brittany 1971'

I had hitched from Calais, or some other godforsaken toilet of a French port, and collected a pleasant Greek traveller en route. He related tales of the military coup in his home country and how he was a staunch dissident and so forth. We got on well – I even learned how to say "I want to eat a railway" in Greek, although I forget how that came about.

We reached Loctudy in the early evening. Trying to save cash and it being warm, we decided to set out our sleeping bags under a large clinker-built fishing boat on the soft sands. We fell asleep but around midnight, I was woken by a shuffling sound. I then saw a pair of polished army-style boots in front of my nose. A gruff voice shouted for us to get up. There was also a sort of rhythmic tapping which accompanied the situation; as we stood up on the beach I found this to be a large studded stick being gently struck into the palm of a hand. We were being confronted by three uniformed members of the CRS riot police unit. We were told it was illegal to sleep on the beach and put under arrest. We were manhandled into a waiting 'meatwagon.' Inside was an array of interesting weaponry, a veritable armoury which included tyre spikes, smoke grenades, machine guns, boxes of ammunition, machetes, cattle prods and many packs (stolen?) of Gauloises.

We were taken to the police station, fingerprinted and pushed into a cell. Our passports had been taken. They asked me a few questions but were simply abusive towards my Greek companion. After about an hour, I was released, given back my passport and sent on my way. It took about an hour to walk back to the beach. I gathered up our belongings from under the boat and waited nearby.

At about 6 am the Greek returned looking awful. He had bruises on his face and was badly shaken. He told me he had been beaten up and questioned by some detectives. Despite repeated questions, he refused to tell me anything else.

I returned to England a week or two later having travelled with the Greek to Amsterdam. I telephoned the Greek Embassy to ask whether my companion was in any danger. He was, an official told me, a wanted dissident. I was politely advised to sever all contact. I did.

# Adrian Jessop  call centre manager
### 'Chercher la Femme'

I used to travel alone a lot of the time. It was just the way it was, but if someone was going my way then you'd team up, of course. One time, I got outside Munich and the best spot was taken by this girl, hitching alone. Not that weird, but she had the spot — a little lay-by and I'd have to wait until she got a lift. It didn't take long for females, so I sat down on the grass nearby – not so near as to cut her chances but near enough to make it obvious I was waiting.

Anyway, a car soon pulled in and I got up to take her place as she dipped into the waiting car. Then she turned around to me and beckoned me over. I was puzzled but went over. She smiled and held the door for me and kind of ushered me in. Needless to say the young guy who had stopped was a little pissed off but he couldn't refuse. I sat in the back, the girl sat in the front and off we went. She turned around and asked me, in English, if I was English (she was Dutch), I said yeah and thanked her for getting me the lift. She said that we were going the same way. Anyway, we hitched together until late that night, the last lift being in a big lorry with an Arab driver. I was in the passenger seat and Tineke, that was her name, was laid out on the driver's bunk just behind. And this Arab guy said to me in French (I spoke French, Tineke didn't), "Can I fuck your girl?" There were a lot of presumptions when you hitched but I couldn't answer for her; I didn't know her well enough to answer for her or to get protective, although I felt that a bit. Anyway, I translated for her, she said to tell him no, she didn't seem upset about it. I was a bit wound-up somehow and I was relieved when we were dropped. As the lorry pulled away she seemed very pissed off with me. Anyway it turned out that she thought I should have whacked the guy or something for even asking and somehow I got the feeling she thought I was complicit in his request. We parted company, better off on my own and yes, the next morning I was back outside hitching alone.

# Bernd Wechner committed hitch-hiker and columnist for Suite101.com

## 'A Christmas Pervert'

I was home for Christmas, and decided to pass the turn of the year, century, millennium, whatever, at an alternative festival on the Murray river. I'd had plans to visit a favourite old haunt (Woodford) with my girl, but that fell through earlier in the year and now I was alone, ruminant. The ConFest seemed as likely a place as any, away from the big cities, where I might find people of like mind.

I set out on Christmas Day. Our family never did celebrate then, adhering to the continental tradition, celebrating the eve before. It struck me as an opportune moment to test the Christmas spirit a little. There wasn't much traffic out, and I had fond memories of a prior Christmas hitch. My brother and his new girl dropped me at the base of a mountain pass heading inland (the Maquarie Pass). It was raining lightly, and they didn't want to leave me there, so far out of town with no certainty of a ride. But it didn't faze me any. What bothered me a little more were the flies that wouldn't stop landing on my face, and the couple parked right here on this desolate little spot as if it were lovers' lane. I felt an urge to say "Happy Christmas" or something, but they evaded eye contact like the plague. They drove off without casting a backward glance, maybe 20 minutes of smooching later. Can't help but wonder what they thought of this hitcher in the rain...

Some while later I needed to take a leak. Left my pack standing there and went over to the bushes. Sure enough, some guy pulls over then and there. He waits till I'm done. Strange guy, strange ride. He was headed to Canberra, and I might have liked to pass through Canberra, but this grandfather couldn't stop talking about getting his end in, head jobs and such. He was convinced I was headed for an orgy for some reason (I think 'alternative lifestyles festival' were my words). This dirty old man thought I was a Christian for some reason, asked me directly and expressed surprise at my denial of such. It's to the credit of Christians, I dare say, that dirty old men like this think that respect of women is inherently Christian.

When I lost him I felt proud of myself. I was keen to get out of this car ASAP and there's a certain art to getting a driver to suggest the best point of exit himself and even insist on it. We simply discussed my route, traffic and such; he knew the road well and we agreed, tactically, that Marulan services weren't far down the road, but definitely my best chance of getting an onward ride to Albury. It's often hard to convince a driver that a short ride to a good spot is better than a long ride to a bad spot.

## Lars Therkildsen historian

My friend and I were hitch-hiking across Europe and reached the Greek-Bulgarian border on a stormy night in April. We were pretty excited about what it would be like, since neither of us had been to an Eastern European country before. We were also a bit nervous regarding our comfort and security though – we had basically no idea of what would greet us on the other side.

It began rather badly. On the Greek side there was a small border control checkpoint we had to go through. Then we were supposed to walk about five hundred metres in no man's land through some trees, over a tiny bridge and then a bit further to the Bulgarian border control post. As we left the building we heard the customs officer saying through his moustache, half to us, half to himself, "Bulgaria? Why on earth do you want to go to Bulgaria?" With that remark on our minds we started crossing no man's land. We then had a very unsettling experience.

When we had almost crossed the bridge, both of us stopped and noticed some kind of large, circular object on the asphalt. It was difficult to see what it was in the failing light. We both began to feel uneasy since the thing was in our way. We warily approached it and noticed that it was a big pool of something black or red. We looked a bit closer: it was blood. A big, thick pool of blood the size of a tractor's wheel. And it smelled really bad. My friend looked very disturbed and neither of us knew what to say or think. Could it have been some poor illegal immigrant trying to cross the border? Or some animal?

"What the hell is going on in this place?" my friend asked. After a few moments we started discussing what we should do. Should we go back? It was getting darker and darker and I had the voice of that Greek customs officer in my head. We agreed it would be stupid not to continue and started walking to the Bulgarian side. We tried not to panic ourselves or the apparently trigger-happy police officers and walked as calmly as possible. We didn't have the guts to ask about the pool of blood when we reached the other side, so we never found out what had happened. I guess someone really had been shot trying to cross the border illegally. Welcome to Eastern Europe, I thought, as we entered the Bulgarian border station.

When we reached this small building we became aware of the administrative and bureaucratic hell that existed in Bulgaria and that we would experience later on in Romania and Hungary regarding our visas. This situation would have made Franz Kafka proud. Three hours of hassle later, we found ourselves in a little Eastern European border village in the middle of the night, wondering what to do.

Once on the Bulgarian side we tried to get a ride with one of the few cars that had found their way to this almost desolate place. But there was no luck. In the end we managed to find the village's one hostel (that only had one room), and slept the rest of the night. Early in the morning, I was woken up by a big shadow flying by outside the window. Only when we left the hostel later in the day, did I discover what it was. On top of almost every chimney and lamp post in the village was a stork's nest, and the big, impressive birds were circling over our heads the whole day.

But we weren't ornithologists and we wanted to go to Sofia. When we asked people where there was a good spot to hitch-hike from or whether they knew anyone that was driving to the capital, they just looked at us as if we were completely insane and shouted, "Train! Train!" Our efforts to explain to them that we preferred hitch-hiking got us nowhere. Maybe they hadn't heard about it. Or maybe they thought it was weird that spoiled kids from Western Europe were too cheap to buy a train ticket. As it turned out they had a point, as when we finally gave in and bought two tickets for the night train to Sofia, it cost us a ridiculously small amount of money. If general prices were this cheap in the East, I could have gone all the way to Siberia with what I had in my wallet.

# A Lift Less Ordinary

# Doug Stanhope comic, optimist and failure

## 'Road Gods'

Some thirty miles outside of Roswell, New Mexico – in the middle of three hundred and sixty degrees of barren desert – the transmission in my Olds Cutlass decided that life was too unbearable and left me and Becker sitting roadside, all thumbs and assholes.

These were the days before AAA and cash to spare. These were the days of gas station sink-showers and the old man's credit card number scrawled on the back of a worn business card in my wallet. Just in case.

The gig is that night in Clovis, about 100 miles north, so I leave Becker to deal with getting the car towed back to Roswell while I pack some overnights out of the trunk and put my thumb out heading north to the show.

Hitch-hiking with such an enviable mullet could be difficult enough in a high-traffic area but now I'm on a road that even tumbleweeds avoid.

I have always been aware of Road Gods, the patron saints of broke comics. There have been too many perfect coincidences to deny it. You run out of gas just as you pull up to the pump. You get a flat tyre right next to the only tyre store for 100 miles. I never once missed a gig. So I had no sense of panic as I stood there on an empty road with nothing but blowing sand passing me by.

And then it came. The first vehicle – maybe the only vehicle on that road at all for all I knew – came into sight and as it got closer we saw that it was a bus.

Not a charter bus – a regular city transit bus like you would find in any large metropolitan area. Like you would find anywhere but out here in the absolute middle of nowhere, 30 miles from the closest town and hundreds of miles from any city that would possibly have a bus. It was like seeing a 7-11 on the moon and before we could say a word about it, the bus slowed to a stop in front of me and the doors opened with a whoosh, like this were a regular stop.

I looked at Becker, Becker looked at me and with nothing but a shrug I got on the bus. The doors whooshed shut and without even having exact change we were on our way.

So it turns out there is a plant in Roswell that makes city buses and this one was being delivered to New York City. And its route from Roswell to the Apple happened to be going right through Clovis, right past the bar where I was performing.

The driver entertained me with tales and observations of his views on faggots, niggers and all the times he came close in life. There's a time and a place to stand up and vocalize your beliefs and there are other times to shut up and nod and enjoy your free ticket out of a fucked place.

Shortly before Showtime, the bus pulled up to its regular stop steps from whatever awful sports bar that was cruel enough to book me and with that familiar whoosh, the doors closed and the bus disappeared as though none of it had ever really happened.

Vultures were most certainly circling over Becker by now – he never had the luck, that guy. He was never young. I had cold beer and ugly girls with hand-curled bangs and I had a really good story – a story that you really had to be there but you have to try to tell it anyway.

## Jeremy Vine broadcaster

In the States, in Texas, I saw a man running along with his thumb out, so I picked him up. He was soaking wet and straight away I wished I hadn't stopped because he was dripping all over the car. I asked him why he had been running and he said, "I was trying to wash in the river down there, and when I surfaced I was staring into the beady eyes of a crocodile. It opened its mouth and I jumped out - I've been running ever since."

## Mike Leigh film director

One time, coming south on the A5 between the M6 and the M1 (they weren't yet connected in those days), I was picked up by a dapper elderly gent in a Sunbeam Talbot.

We drove along for a while in silence. Then suddenly he said, "Can I tell you something?"

I asked him what he meant, and he said he'd just had a traumatic experience, and if he told me now, a stranger, then he'd have got it off his chest, and he'd never have to tell anyone else.

I was probably about 20 at this time. I told him I'd be happy to share his experience, and he proceeded to describe how he'd just been to see an old friend of his, whom he was in the habit of visiting from time to time. Both men were married, the two couples going back to before the Second World War.

So he drops in, shares a cup of tea with his old crony, and passes the time of day. Then his friend says, "Can I show you something?"

"What d'you want to show me?"

"I'm going upstairs, wait here and come up when I call you."

So he waits, and after a few minutes, he gets the call. He climbs the stairs slowly. His friend calls, "In here...."

And he goes into the bedroom and there's his friend – "dressed as a woman!"

Stunned, he says no, of course he doesn't mind. Then our cross-dresser gets changed, and asks him to keep it to himself, because it's a secret – even his wife doesn't know.

Then the gentleman takes his leave, drives off, and picks me up.

Cut to me, getting out, thanking him for the lift, and holding up my thumb for the next mad motorist.

# Michael Crick journalist and broadcaster

I used to hitch thousands of miles a year when I was a teenager in the 1970s. This was mainly following Manchester United around the country from my home in Stockport. I became so skilled at knowing where to stand, what routes to take, and how to time my journeys, that over the course of about four years going to every match, I only missed one fixture through failing to get lifts and not getting there on time. Mind you, that was in the days of traditional Saturday afternoon three o'clock kick-offs. Today's hotchpotch fixture list would present many more problems.

Nor was it always easy getting home to Stockport on Saturday night, especially in winter when it gets dark early. Many a time I would be stuck next to some remote motorway junction in the freezing cold and fog (of an intensity which no longer seems to exist and which prevented any driver seeing you). And there was always this dilemma: should I use my traditional red and white United scarf to keep warm, or would that put drivers off giving me lifts?

Perhaps my most extraordinary experience occurred in March 1973, after we'd won 3-1 at Chelsea in London. I was running late, and glad to get picked up around 11pm at Watford Gap on the M1, a favourite hitching spot just before the motorway divides into the M1 and M6. Once I got talking to the driver, he explained he was a zoologist who specialized in venomous snakes.

"Oh," I said, half-nervously and half-joking, "I hope you haven't got any in the car."

He hesitated a moment and said, "No."

But then he announced that he was thinking of visiting a friend, somewhere off the A5 near Tamworth, who had an excellent collection of deadly reptiles. Would I be interested in coming along? Of course I was interested, and in any case it didn't seem I had much option if I wasn't to lose my lift. But it seemed an odd thing to do at that time of night.

The zoologist's friend was a bit eccentric, to say the least. He lived in a large hut, surrounded by snakes of all kinds, and even had a couple of small rattlesnakes living in glass cabinets next to his bed. The snake man then took one of his creatures out and asked if I'd like to hold it. No way. How would the snake react if I dropped it in terror? I was rather more brave when the reptile-keeper took me into his humid alligator room at the back of the building, where one of the 'gators was snoozing in a small pool with its head resting on the bank. I must have only been standing about four feet from its jaws as the keeper prodded the creature with a stick to wake him up. Fortunately he didn't seem interested in devouring me for supper.

It all seemed so bizarre. As if it was quite normal for someone to live in a hut surrounded by snakes. And perfectly ordinary for a friend to drop by and inspect them in the middle of the night.

The zoologist had actually come to collect one particular snake. The two men pulled it out of its cage, dropped it into a brown canvas bag and tied the bag tightly with string. The driver then nonchalantly placed the bag on the back seat of the car. With that, we continued on our journey.

# Herb Fenway music producer
### 'The Trenchtown Amnesiac'

I was standing in the centre of an outdoor Jamaican dancehall, demarcated from the rest of the beach with dim lanterns and tower blocks of speakers. A wobbling, impossibly bass-heavy wave of music poured from a DJ booth at the far end, drenching every patron with the urge to dance in painstaking slow motion, heads bowed and limbs arching.

I was enjoying myself immensely. This was the one thing I wanted to experience on my trip to Jamaica: *bona fide* Jamaican dub in a *bona fide* Jamaican setting. Back home I'd heard only tantalizing morsels of this new, exotic rebel music. My only concern was that I had no memory of how I'd got here. The last I recalled I was sitting down on the roadside near Trenchtown, feeling drained and pissed off as I had run out of money the moment I had bought the bus ticket from Kingston to Trenchtown. But this whole trip had been a frenzy of fun and improvisation, involving little certainty or forward-planning. I resolved to continue having fun and not ask myself awkward questions.

Max Romeo's now legendary 'War Ina Babylon' came on; the buzz of recognition and my fifth rum and coke spurred me to take my dancing more seriously. As I ambled nearer to the bombastic source of the music, a trio of rude boys caught my eye. They were wild-eyed, sharp-suited, flat-capped and keeping to themselves beside the bar. They didn't seem to like my squarejohn appearance and ungainly bopping, so I turned away from them and approached two beautiful girls in tribal headgear. I goofily and rudely tried to enter their conversation but they just smiled and shook their heads at me, doing wonders for my sense of self-worth. I turned away from them too and spotted the rude boys who were once again sizing me up. The whole crowd now seemed to be aiming disapproving looks at me and I half-expected the DJ to cut the music and exhort everybody to laugh me out of the dancehall.

Thankfully this didn't happen but worryingly one of the rude boys broke from his throng and approached me. He had one eyebrow raised in a menacing fashion. He looked exceedingly 'bling bling' (to use contemporary parlance) in his perfectly-tailored zoot suit and snow-white brothel creepers.

"You gaan buy me drink?"

I didn't think that I'd heard him over the sludgy thudding of the world's greatest music.

"I'm sorry," I replied, trying not to sound like a clueless tourist. I failed. He repeated himself very slowly.

"Are you goin' to buy me drink, man?"

I frowned, disappointed by the man's overt begging. "Why should I?"

"After what I done for you?"

"What?"

"After all I done for you, man?" He accentuated the "all" as if he'd saved me from an earthquake or low-level nuclear assault.

I lost my temper. "FUCK OFF!" I yelled and then closed my eyes, feeling my face fill with a crimson blush. "I'm sorry," I said to the rude boy, whose eyes were growing wider and angrier. "I don't understand..."

He put his arm round me. I flinched before realising he was being conciliatory. He led me to the far edge of the hall, where a dwarf in a string vest and dog-tags was selling pre-rolled joints laid out on a rickety coffee table. The music was quieter here.

The rude boy leaned towards my ear. I was on the verge of soiling myself.

"Me c'yan believe you so ungrateful, man. I picked you up in Trenchtown. You was asleep by de road an' my frien's me were 'fraid you be robbed by bandits. So we lifted you into de car and drove you here, right. Or did you forget?"

So that was what had happened to me during my period of memory loss. I did remember being on the roadside near the station for some time and feeling pretty tired. The relief took off from my shoulders like an albatross.

"Yes I'm so sorry. I did forget. What are you drinking?"

# John Bartlett sometime itinerant player and follower of Thespis!

1970! School's out for summer and college is yet to begin. Oh, the optimism of youth, everything to live for and everything to gain; nothing could stand in our way! Hitch our way across Europe or even around the world; in the event we settled for Devon and Cornwall!

There were four of us in all, Lester, Dave, Pongo or sometimes Pengis and myself. We set off one hot day in August walking along the dusty road by the railway station that leads to Winchester and beyond. We decided that a party of four was unlikely to succeed and that pairs were a much better proposition. So be it, Lester and Pongo set off together leaving Dave and I to bring up the rear – so far so good!

What ensued next was a hitch-hiker's nightmare - a sequence of lifts for a mile or two; madly waving at our unfortunate fellow hitch-hiking travellers as we hurtled by, only to be overtaken a mile or two down the road. This state of affairs went on for most of the day until finally both parties parted company not to be seen again, or so we thought. Having travelled all of forty-eight miles in ten hours, Dave and I were putting our best foot forward when up ahead we noticed the gait of two familiar figures. Ha! Ha! So we hadn't been left behind after all! Comradeship restored, we decided to pitch our tent, or what loosely passed for a tent, in a nearby cornfield. Fresh out of school having recently been forced to watch a survival film, it was decided to employ the tactics of the S.A.S. and fill the tent full of corn to provide a buffer between the ground and us. Feeling very proud of ourselves we then headed off for the nearest pub.

Several hours later we returned to find the interior of the tents crawling with what can only be described as alien life forms that had somehow managed to 'beam down' choosing our pitiful hovels as cover for their nefarious activities! A cold, itchy and sleepless night ensued to the sound of lorries thundering past, any one of which could have taken us to the distant 'Promised Land', The West Country!

The next day we arose bleary-eyed, stiff and sore, but relatively cheerful. The various itchy welts were compared and admired and with no real harm done we were on our way once more. Four hours later neither team had moved an inch, so a temporary adjournment to a nearby hostelry was called for. After a liquid lunch we set to with a will, to no avail. Eventually we took it in turns to stick out a lethargic thumb whilst the other slept under our pile of belongings.

"John, we've got a lift!" came the excited cry! I don't think I have ever moved so quickly and before the driver knew what was going on we were both crammed in the back of the car with tents, sleeping bags and the remainder of our gear.

"Where are you going?" asked the driver.

"Cornwall" we hopefully replied.

"Well I can take you as far as St Austell, will that do?"

Elation knew no bounds; we were finally really on our way. For a short while we felt the pangs of guilt as both of us knew that Lester and Pongo had been left behind. It later transpired, as they had been in pole position, seeing us get a lift before them; they gave up and returned home. What a shame! However, quickly putting our guilt aside, we at least were winging our way west, youthfully wondering what the real relationship was between the driver and his beautiful Italian companion.

Once we had arrived, nothing particularly happened and we managed to get lifts fairly easily. That is until two or three days into our adventure, we were walking up the main high street of St Ives and, unexpectedly, some school friends were walking down the other way! Greeting each other like long-lost buddies with a "Dr Livingstone, I presume!"

We all enthusiastically shook hands and retired to the nearest hostelry to celebrate. It turned out that Guy and companions had set off at more or less the same time as we had, the only difference being that they had 'wheels' and without their camping gear there was room for us! Now we could explore with style and explore we did: Land's End, Mousehole, Penzance, you name it, we went there. On one occasion it was decided to look up our old art teacher, Neddie Naden, who had recently retired to 'Slip Cottage', which was situated in the middle of the china clay mining area, known locally as 'Little Switzerland' on account of the white snow-like appearance of the towering slag heaps.

Not knowing exactly where to find 'Slip Cottage', I was volunteered to knock on the door of a humble, but well-kept dwelling to ask the way. After boldly knocking on the door I waited for a response; after some time the door opened and I was greeted by a friendly, weather-beaten face, balancing precariously on top of a crooked and gnarled old body. I explained our predicament, which took a little while to sink in, but once he had repeated everything once or twice, this worthy old gent explained, in an accent you could cut bread with, that I was to go down the road, turn right and take the first on the left. "Yep," he said. "Go down the road, turn right and take the first on the left."

"Thank you very much," I said.

Assuming that I probably needed telling again, he proceeded with a ..... "Yep, go down the road, turn right and take the first on the left."

Thanking him profusely once more, I attempted to rejoin my impatient friends in the car. This country worthy, having warmed to the subject, was not to going to be put off that easily and was about to give me directions for a fourth time, when his equally aged wife made her way to the front door. As her ancient partner had been gone for some time, she, of course, wanted to know what on earth was going on.

"Argh well, this young gent wants to know where Slip Cottage is."

"Slip Cottage?" the old lady mused. "You've got to go down the road, turn right and take the first on the left."

"That's right," said my octogenarian friend. "Go down the road, turn right and take the first on the left".

This state of affairs went on for some time before, somewhat bemused, but definitely on the right track, I was finally allowed to go on my way! ... God bless them both!

**Jon Grover** works as a reporter and dog musher in Bethel, Alaska but always has an eye towards the road system and his next ride

### 'An Unusual Hitch'

I had moved to Bethel, a small town in rural Alaska, with no roads in or out. An old friend from college, Paul, had convinced me to move there and work as a dog musher. I had already decided to leave my home in Upstate New York, but my intention was to hitch around the States for a while.

Despite knowing that moving to Alaska would mean putting the brakes on my wanderin' ways for a time, I decided to take him up and experience the adventure that I figured was pretty much guaranteed as a musher in the "last great frontier".

I never expected to hitch one of the most extreme rides of my life in a place with virtually no roads.

One afternoon in February, Paul and I hitched up two dog teams and set out on the trail. It was a cold, clear day and trail conditions were perfect.

With eight dogs shooting me across the frozen lakes and tundra I was in heaven. Paul had a smaller team with six dogs and couldn't keep up, so I stopped to wait for him.

Suddenly, my normally cool headed lead dog, Big One, heard Paul's team coming up the trail from behind and spooked. He turned on the trail and bolted back the way we had come; in the process he knocked me off the sled. I tried to catch up, but it was hopeless. I couldn't hope to run down a team of eight dogs, so I shouted for Paul in hopes that he could stop them on the trail but it was too late, the dogs were too fast.

Paul's team spun on him too and he held tight to the sled, giving chase to my team. I was alone...about eight miles from town. It was about twenty-five below zero, but I was dressed warm and had a full pack of smokes, so I started walking and singing.

I walked for some time, a few miles, singing, smoking and squinting to avoid snow-blindness. I was bundled up, which helped with the cold, but made for difficult walking and I started to get pretty tired.

As I started across one of many frozen lakes, I heard a snow machine coming. Instinctively, I stuck out my thumb, hoping for a lift back to town. The man slowed, obviously confused how I came to be so far from town on foot in February, the coldest month of the year.

When he came to a stop I saw a gun slung over each shoulder and another in a holster strapped to the machine. Embarrassed, I explained that I had been victimized by a berzerk dog-team and, after a few laughs at my expense, he told me to hop on the back.

Relieved and tired, I climbed on for the fast, bumpy ride back home. There was no problem crossing the myriad of lakes; the excitement came with the high speeds this hunter chose to rocket over the tundra trails: each bump would send his guns swinging to and fro, waving in my face.

Before long, though, he was dropping me off in the dog yard, safe enough and lesson learned. Don't let go of the dog sled. And sitting right there in front of their houses were eight dogs, smiling as if to say "Wasn't that fun?"

# Michael Rosen writer and broadcaster

In France, I was trying to get from Carcassonne to Perpignan with my friend Dave. We were seventeen. A 2CV stopped and the driver was a chubby man in a black woollen shirt, glasses. He spoke with a deep musical voice. We talked in French.

I said that we wanted to go to Perpignan. He said that he was going to Perpignan in a couple of days' time, why didn't we come back to his place up in the mountains? I asked him his job and he said he was a priest, a curé. "Are you shocked?" he asked.

"No," I said. I wasn't shocked but he wasn't wearing the clothes of a curé. He explained that he chose not to. He said that he was a priest in a small village up in the mountains. "You might be shocked. In the houses there's no water or toilets."

We travelled up and up and up and then on to some kind of plateau with the peaks still above us. Then we took a tiny lane that wiggled across the plain and down what seemed like a crack in the ground to a village. "This is Espezel," he said. "The people here don't really speak French. They speak patois."

His house was an old stone farmhouse, next to the church. Inside, he had a vase full of teasels and big black and white pictures of the sides of buildings and bas-reliefs from the cloister at Elne. He scarcely had any furniture apart from a couple of old wooden chairs and tables. He said we could stay with him and he would take us out to show us what life was like for the peasants in the high Pyrenees. So for a couple of days he drove us out and around. He showed us the village cemetery and explained that for the peasants it was a fetish. Death for them was a cult. It was a carry-over from pagan times. He showed us some tiny fields of grass that were almost vertical.

"You see those posts?" he said. "The peasants tie themselves to those posts and lower themselves down so that they can cut the hay. Then they wrap it up in huge bundles and carry them back to their barns, the women as well as the men."

Out on the road, we saw one old woman, tiny under a huge bundle of hay, just as he said, and he waved and shouted to her and she grunted back.

The next day, he said he was going to go up to the lake, and asked did we want to come? Dave didn't, but I went. Once we were there, he said that he was going to sunbathe. Did I want to? I said, no, I didn't like sunbathing. "Do you mind if I take off all my clothes?" he asked.

"No, no, you go ahead," I said.

So he took off all his clothes and showed his chubby pink body to the sun. I walked about, throwing stones and trying to catch flying grasshoppers. He said he was going to read some Teilhard de Chardin. Had I ever heard of Teilhard de Chardin?

"No," I said.

"You would be very interested in him," he said. "He is both very modern and very ancient in his thinking. I think he is very important for Catholics."

I listened without looking at him and mooched off again. Then he put his clothes back on and said that we would go back now. In the car, he asked me if I was shocked that he had taken his clothes off.

"No, no," I said, "That's fine."

## Carrie Wiltshire

My friend Jane and I, with freshly cashed gyros, decided we were bored, so we set ourselves a challenge of seeing how fast we could hitch from John O'Groats to Lands End. We were on our way up to John O'Groats, but got stuck about 10 miles outside. We were sitting on the roadside in the drizzle, with our rucksacks and tent, sheltering under our umbrella, when a funeral cortege passed in the opposite direction. We were still there when they were on their way back and, to our amazement (of course we hadn't stuck our thumbs out), they stopped and offered us a lift in the limo. It was quite bizarre. By the way, we did the John O'Groats to Lands End trip non-stop in twenty-six hours – any tales of a faster journey?

## Arnold Wesker playwright/director

I hitch-hiked everywhere. Once, aged fifteen, I was struck with an idea I thought would double the sales of Kelloggs Cornflakes. My idea was: let it be known that in certain packets there would be a card saying you had won £5, £10, £15 every five up to a £1000. I couldn't see how everyone would not instantly buy two or three packets of Cornflakes. When I get an idea I have to act on it instantly. My parents were at work. I left them a note saying I was hitch-hiking to Manchester to make my fortune. Of course I was treated kindly by an official from the firm who said it was an idea they had contemplated, naturally, but there was a law preventing such a ploy.

## James Hobbs journalist

A friend – the kind of vegan who won't buy vegetables from a greengrocer who eats meat – found herself stranded with her boyfriend in the Australian outback when their car broke down. Help eventually came, but it is hard to know how else she would have come to meet the man who gave them a lift: a kangaroo hunter whose pick-up was overflowing with carcasses.

# Patrons and Passengers

## Mike Leigh film director

In the sixties, we all hitched everywhere. We hardly ever took a train or a bus. Living in London, I'd hitch up to Manchester to see my parents, or to Glasgow or Liverpool to see mates. I once hitched from London to Marseilles in six days to catch an ancient Turkish boat to the Holy Land, where I worked on a kibbutz.

On that trip I got stuck with a very thick unemployed young guy from Paisley. He was called Wilson McDougal. He wore a kilt and being all alone on the Continent was about the last thing he was cut out for.

We started hitching together in the pouring rain on the road from Boulogne to Paris. Our first lift was an elderly and mildly irate posh English lady in a Morris Traveller (the half-timbered version of the Morris Minor). She was from the Lake District, and lectured us for an hour on how what we were doing created a bad image of Great Britain. Then she dropped us off during a thunderstorm.

Our luck changed. A charming, youngish guy in a big Citroën gave us a lift to Paris, picked up his gorgeous young Parisian wife, with whom I instantly fell in love, and took us out for dinner. Then they put us up in the spare room of their tiny apartment.

Mr McDougal remained out of his depth in all aspects of this experience, not least in matters of etiquette, conversation, gastronomy and hygiene, and I managed to give him the slip the next day near the Gare du Nord. Thirty years later, he was the inspiration for Ewen Bremner's character 'Archie' in my film *Naked*.

There were dozens of hitching adventures on the Continent. The most memorable on that trip was the obvious ex-Nazi (this was 1961), who was happy to give a lift to a Dutch guy I'd fallen in with, but not me. We'd told him we were both heading for Marseilles to catch the Haifa-bound *SS Istanbul*, and he'd asked us both, "Sind Sie Juden?" The Dutch guy wasn't Jewish, but I admitted I was. End of story. I had to make alternative arrangements.

# Michael Rosen writer and broadcaster

I was on the A1 coming home from Leeds when two guys picked me up. They were giggling and nudging each other. They seemed to be laughing about the fact that they didn't really know how to drive the car. The one not driving was making suggestions as to how change gear but he didn't really know much more than the driver. You know the sort of thing: "Fourth is over there, up and across…" Every now and then, one of them would say things like: "Nice covers on the seats." "Nice dash." And the like. They seemed to be getting a feel of the car for the first time. It wasn't new – it seemed quite old, a second-hand Hillman.

After a while, the driver said that they would have to go off to see some friends, then come back on to the A1 in a while. Did I want to come with them, or get off ? I always worked to the theory that a car in the hand was worth two zooming past the bushes, so I said I'd stay on. We drove off the A1 into the open flatlands of middle England. We left surfaced roads, and went on to farm tracks. They seemed to be getting a little excited, a little anxious. It had been a sunny day but it was now beginning to get dark.

After a bit more driving along tracks, through the open dried-out fields we arrived at some old broken-down farm buildings. But it didn't look like any farm I knew, more like a set of garages. A guy came out in his overalls and looked at me. My two guys just grinned and waved me aside, saying that they had picked me up on the A1. The driver turned round and said that this was where they mended their vehicles. They asked me if I wanted to get out of the car. I said that I'd rather stay where I was and I watched them go off with the overalls guy and look into some of the old buildings. They went in and out, nodding and laughing. I have a memory that amongst the buildings was an old army tank. I'm not absolutely sure if this was the case or if I've invented it. I seem to remember that it was beat-up and rusted but loomed over us all.

After yet more time, the guys got back into the car, we drove back through the fields, on to the surfaced roads and back to the A1. They asked me what I did and thought it was a gas that I was a student. "We guessed as much," they said. They asked, as nearly all drivers did who picked me up in the sixties, what the girls were like. They always seemed to want to know if we were at it all the time or most of the time. They dropped me off at Apex Corner and I saw them drive off, still stalling the car, and worrying about how to drive it.

# Gary Gygax creator of *Dungeons & Dragons*

Most of what I did was 'goosing a ghost' to get to nearby towns when I should have been in school. The pool hall in Burlington was a regular destination. Getting rides to any place around here wasn't easy, then when someone would pick us up it was often only a short ride along the route, so a good deal of the distance between communities was often walked.

About the only vaguely interesting lift I can recall was when a friend, Phil Gray, and I were hitching to get to Williams Bay, a small community on Lake Geneva about five miles distance from the city of Lake Geneva. A middle-aged chap in a caddy with two young lady companions, surely his nieces, gave us a ride. He asked us what we thought of his girlfriends, but at around age fourteen we were far too backwards and shy to say anything at all.

# Genevieve Gilchrist

Trouble with tales is that everyone has their own perception. I spoke to one of my partners in hitching and he remembered being cold and walking a lot when I remembered being lucky – that's how it is. All I can offer you is my lucky story.....

It was New Year's Eve. Muffy always had THE BEST parties at New Year so my sister, Boc, brother-in-law by a different sister, Berg, and I decided, on the day, we should go up to Reading.

There is no snow on Hayling Island, something to do with salt in the air – bit of a bummer when you're growing up because snowballs and snowmen are elusive and schools never close in the winter. Still we left, quite well-wrapped and brave.

It was a strange time, probably not that special but a new time for Britain. Thatcher was making her mark and we were very much on the down side of the divide – we would have felt more at home north of Sheffield but we were living in the affluent end of southern suburban england (with a small e), broke and bearing the new wealth brunt as best we could.

We didn't have to wait long for the first lift, or speak – the driver was considerate and quiet – an unusual trait in Britain at that time because everyone felt as though they had a right to shout and stamp on others. It was a mean and selfish era.

He dropped us at the next roundabout which was inland, enough, for the snow to start laying and staying and we were cold – fucking cold, hanging about waiting, watching, wishing when suddenly a low, fast car stopped. I don't know about cars but I know you or anyone would have been impressed by this one (unless of course you're like me, a non driver and eco friendly! not many around at that time).

Still I was impressed. I was cold and it was getting so late we were going to miss midnight. He drove so fucking fast. He was in a suit and he had another one hanging up in the rear of the car so that Boc and I had to move it aside so that we could see. He didn't talk very much but you could smell from his aftershave that he was one of the Thatcher boys making money on the backs or on their backs. It was easy for us. Safety in numbers. We were going nowhere really – just to a party – not trying to prove anything and there must have been something – some connection – some bravery on both parts for him to have stopped.

I don't remember what we said – I just knew that he knew that we were from the other side – politically, socially, morally, but it was New Year's Eve; he was driving to London and suddenly he did a detour to Reading.

Berg kept talking to the driver and I started to think his aftershave smelt pretty good – it reminded me of a French teacher I had when I was ten.

He dropped us on the Reading roundabout and we had quite a bit of walking to do after that but it was way out of his way. As we climbed out of his low, fast car he leant into the back and pulled out a bottle of Jack Daniels.

"Happy New Year – this might keep you from getting cold – have a drink on me."

We walked and drank and I forgave the whole of Britain or mostly southern england for having being taken in by Maggie T., though any number of Jack Daniels would never let me forgive *her*.

So we walked then and this is the part that Berg remembers (different perceptions?). We eventually got to the party well before midnight. Strange because Muffy is the daughter of a millionaire who has something to do with scaffolding. Her house (one of them) in Reading was wall-to-wall antiques but tonight full of her son's friends who were indiscriminately indifferent to antiques – punks, glue-sniffers and the one that put his fag out on the oak sideboard was extremely sexy. Isn't that what New Year's Eve and politics are all about?

# Robert Bateman artist, environmentalist and Officer of the Order of Canada

In 1957-58, my wildlife biologist friend Bristol Foster and I went around the world in a Landrover. We travelled across tropical Africa, northern India and through parts of southeast Asia and Australia. It was still partly colonial (Belgian Congo and the Kenya colony) and was perfectly safe compared to many parts of the route today. We slept in the Landrover every night and cooked most of our own meals.

Instead of driving through the Middle East we sailed, third class, on an Indian passenger ship from Mombasa to Bombay. As we drove out of Bombay we picked up a young Englishman who was hitch-hiking.

When we asked him how far he was going he gave the dreaded reply, "I don't know. How far are you going?"

Instead of lying, we told him that we were going to Calcutta and so he said that was where he was going. This meant that we had a third man for our two month crossing of India.

When I am travelling abroad I like to read fiction based on the place I'm visiting. This seems to permeate my inner being with what my eyes are seeing and I am more fully 'there'. Unfortunately, the book I chose for this part of the journey was John Masters' *The Deceivers*, a true tale of the cult of Thuggee: the original thugs that ambushed travellers at their night encampments, strangled them, robbed them and buried them in shallow graves. My evening readings made me unsettled even in the daytime, especially since there were military roadblocks as a result of the presence of bandits in the area through which we were passing.

Although we tried to camp in out of the way places each evening, we always had an audience of curious locals. Sometimes a couple of dozen people watched us cook supper, eat, brush our teeth and go to bed. They were always back before breakfast in the morning.

One night we were determined to hide in a seemingly remote woodlot and finish our domestic duties before the light faded so we wouldn't give ourselves away with the interior vehicle lights. We were just settling down on our first audience-free night in India when we heard men's voices in the distance. They sounded angry. As they came closer they sounded angrier and we hoped that they would pass by without noticing us. But no, we were their destination. They surrounded the vehicle carrying torches, sticks and clubs.

Our hitch-hiker, who always slept beside the Landrover since there was no room inside, jumped out of his sleeping bag and joined us inside. The leader, a scrawny man with a hawk-like face and a stubble beard tried reaching inside. We had turned on our light hoping that they would view us as innocent travellers. Of course they did not understand English and so in desperation to communicate, I tried mimicking some of their loudest shouts. Eventually someone snickered, perhaps at my pronunciation, then there was a laugh and the whole crowd relaxed in merriment and melted away into the darkness. After a safe interval our hitch-hiker went back out to his sleeping bag and found, not surprisingly, that his passport and wallet were missing. He had brought his money belt into the vehicle.

It was then that we learned that his money belt was full of counterfeit Queen Victoria gold sovereigns. While hitch-hiking from England he had stopped in Afganistan to work for an American construction company. He was told that if he put his earnings into this form of gold and smuggled it into India he could double or triple his money. India had been independent for eleven years but the average person did not yet trust Indian banks and would prefer to keep their savings under the bed in the form of gold. I guess that they trusted Queen Victoria for some reason, but the Indian government strongly frowned on the practice. Our hitch-hiker arrived just in time for the crackdown on gold smuggling. His contact in Bombay had just committed suicide and he was advised to get out of town because if anyone knew he was smuggling gold they could tip off the police and get half the take, and of course the smuggler would spend a very long time in an Indian jail. So now we had a 'hot' passenger who had no passport, no cash, but lots of illicit gold.

The rest of our trip to Calcutta was delightful, interesting and uneventful but we knew that the crunch would come when our hitch-hiker tried to cash in his booty. Through a contact with an Anglican Church in Toronto, we were allowed to camp in a wooded and fenced park surrounding an Anglican church in the heart of Calcutta – an oasis of tranquillity with giant banyan trees, birds and monkeys, in the sea of cars and crowds and rickshaws and noise all around us.

Our hitch-hiker set off with one counterfeit sovereign and approached a rickshaw boy to try out a deal. He was led through a labyrinth of alleys to a door and then several other doors. The 'dealer' he eventually reached was unimpressed. He even bit the sovereign as in the old movies, pronounced it counterfeit and offered our hitch-hiker, instead of double, half what he paid for it. And so there was no deal but the dealer would be motivated to follow our Englishman in hopes of a main cache and a reward of half the take. Bristol and I were anxiously sitting with the booty. We ran a great risk of having the Landrover confiscated and ending up with a long stay in an Indian jail.

Our hitch-hiker used evasive action returning to our churchyard sanctuary and so we were not caught at that moment. Bristol and I and our Landrover joined a Japanese freighter and sailed on to Burma. We wished our English hitch-hiker a fond farewell as we fervently wished him good luck.

# Maia Mongia general practitioner
### 'Tour of Sicily'

Great lifts with priests and doctors, lawyers, really interesting people... a real education. But the best was an old guy in Sicily with the oldest truck in the world. My boyfriend and I were just waiting in the sun and hitching for the very few cars which came by, it was hot and so bright. Away in the distance this old truck came towards us but it took about half an hour to get to us! Eventually it stopped right by us. We had plenty of time to think about the possibility of it stopping and whether it was worth taking the lift. You could be picky in those days.

At the wheel was this ancient guy, like out of a film, all shrivelled and toothless. He kept saying stuff to us which we couldn't understand and seemed to invite us in. So we got in and we chugged off at a snail's pace. He just talked, slowly and lyrically, whilst waving a hand here and there. Sometimes he would just stop the truck and point away to some mountain or villa or to trees or fields and then he seemed to be explaining things – the odd thing was that I was carried along with it. As he pointed at something or looked directly at me as he talked, I really thought I understood – not the words, but the meaning. By the time he dropped us, he had taken us a good few kilometres, before turning off the road. He gave us a lump of bread, some olives and half a bottle of wine from his own lunch basket. We felt very privileged – humbled. So we got a tour of that bit of the coast, in Italian. Didn't understand a word, but learned all about it nevertheless – I'm sure he knew that.

# Steven Pinker Johnstone Family Professor of Psychology at Harvard University

When I was a teenager, hitch-hiking was a big part of my life. I lived in the suburbs of Montreal, and every weekend an impatient friend and I would hitch-hike downtown rather than endure the hour-long bus ride. Usually we were successful, but one afternoon no one would stop, and we thought that two hippies might seem too intimidating. It was autumn, and every lawn sported a huge leaf pile. My friend buried himself in a leaf pile, I stuck my thumb out, and when a car stopped, he rose out of the leaves and joined me in the car.

While a student at McGill University, I continued to live with my parents, and commuted to school by thumb. It was a close-knit Jewish suburb, and the adults would happily pick up a nice boy to keep in touch with the younger generation, catch up on gossip, or find a prospective husband for their daughter.

## Arthur Brown Crazy World of Arthur Brown

A callow youth of 16 in the north of England. Leeds, which is now 'The Gateway to the North' was then all trams, dirt, and Rugby League. I'd never been abroad – unless you count two weeks in the heart of Scotland with the cadet corps, visiting The Black Watch.

I wanted adventure. It came through the agency of a girl – Margaret Jackson. She was my true love of the time. Why, we'd actually kissed and I'd met her mother. She went to Germany – by train. She left me the address to write to. My heart ached for her and I resolved to get to her by fair means or foul. I had heard of hitch-hiking and decided to try my luck.

I set off on my great adventure. Soon I had found my first lift in the back of a family's car with the young children. After two more rides from different people, I finally crossed the channel. I was to stay, I decided, at youth hostels. I soon fell in with savoury and unsavoury types.

A soldier, who was the first man I ever saw who shaved his head, befriended me. He had just come back from the conflict in Cyprus. He could see I was wet behind the ears in spite of my aloof Quiet Man pose. He got me out of several sticky situations before going his own way.

I bought a pair of shoes (for walking in) - brown floaters with a lot of room in them. That was close to Koln. As the Second World War was only recently over it felt quite daring to be in 'enemy territory.' I was enjoying the freedom and the excitement. I was also looking forward to the surprise on Margaret's face when I got to Hamburg.

Instead, it was me who was surprised. When the door opened, it was my best friend Keith who stood in front of me. I had known he was going there, but it was to see his German girlfriend. Margaret said she was most impressed at my getting there on my own – but I knew it was over.

After a couple of days at the house of Keith's ex (who was far too mature for me), having been shown the docks, and the beginning of new growth in Germany, I set off home.

I felt a little defeated, but impressed by German hospitality. There was no animosity where I went. So I carried a good memory of the people there. A loud voice was shouting in German. Soon I realised it was coming from a German police car. They were shouting at me through a loud-speaker. They were on the other side of the autobahn. Autobahn – a huge snaking wide road with a fantastic surface – bigger than anything I'd seen in England. Fast. Efficient. And not crowded. All the same I thought I'd better move away as the police seemed to be upset. I wandered off the road and followed its path behind some trees.

I finally got to a place where I could come back to the road – it was some kind of wayside inn. A local who spoke English told me that the police were probably telling me it was illegal to hitch on the autobahn. Thank goodness I picked up that something was wrong.

At the inn this kind man persuaded an army lorry driver and his mate to give me a ride even though it was illegal to pick up on the autobahn. We drove for many a mile before stopping at another inn for nourishment. No sooner were we sitting comfortably than a jeep squealed to a halt. Out sprang the military police. The one in command screamed at the driver of the vehicle I'd been in. Quickly he told me they had been torn off a strip for giving me a lift in an army vehicle – breaking the civil law. He jumped in his cab and drove off with a sheepish look on his face. I sat at the table, wondering what to do. I was miles away from anywhere where I could hitch, and my funds were getting low.

The MP came over to my table and said, "Where are you going to?"

I explained I was *en route* back to England.

He said, indicating to the jeep, "Get in!" He was smiling a pleasant smile. He indicated that I should get in the rear and lie down. He seemed so pleasant, I did as he suggested. When I lay down he smiled at me conspiratorially, and covered me with a blanket. I was invisible now.

The engine revved and we were off. He drove for an hour or so. Then the car stopped and the blanket was removed. They had brought me a long way along my route. He told me if I went a little over there I would find a road which would get me home fast. One where it was legal to hitch. We said our goodbyes and off they went with a smile.

The rest of my journey was uneventful and I arrived home – a well-travelled and much wiser young man.

# Alex Mitchell   retired police officer
### 'First Time – Last Time'

I was hitching with a friend and we had been to Bournemouth for a few days on the piss. We were only about sixteen or seventeen and we didn't have any money because we'd spent it all on beer. I had my first-ever kebab in Bournemouth and I threw up all over the place. Horrible, it made me ill and I didn't touch kebabs for years after. We got a lift along the M27 to the services at Southampton with some old boy who was just really strange. The conversation was going really weird and weary and we thought, hello, we've either got an axe murderer or some sex pest driving us along. So we made the excuse that we were busting for a piss and we needed to go in the services. So he took us in the services and we both went in to the loos, making sure we lugged our huge rucksacks. We made sure he couldn't see where we were and then legged it because he came looking for us, thinking we'd got lost. He probably thought these poor boys are going to be left. Wonder what's happened to them, probably been abducted... We were hiding from him. Everywhere he was going, we were running round avoiding him, with these two huge rucksacks, hiding behind cars and trucks and trying to keep away from him. After about an hour he gave up and left.

We got a lift with a family after that – bit of a tight squeeze but better than the axe murderer/sex pest. I'm sure he was a nice old chap really.

# Sergi Arnone
## 'The Night Before Canada'

I got picked up by a family. They crammed me in somehow amongst their children and their dog. I was coming back from Canterbury, I think, and they took me to Brighton or Lewes, I can't remember. Anyway it turned out that they were emigrating to Canada the next day and they were really excited and upbeat. They insisted on taking me to the station and giving me the money for the train home. We all said this emotional goodbye to each other – we'd only met an hour before! They were in sentimental mode I suppose and gave me a tenner as well. Off I went to the ticket office and off they went. But I was an exchange student and only had about five pounds a week to live on then, so I kept the train fare and carried on hitching. I hope they had a good time.

# Arnold Wesker   playwright/director

I was once hitch-hiking with a younger cousin and we'd run out of money. A sweet Southern Counties lady with a child picked us up and listened to my lamentations about our hunger. My theatrical performance finally got to her and she stopped to reach into her shopping bag for a cake of which I'd never heard before – a Battenburg cake. It was an oblong box shape, which when cut through revealed a slice of four quarters in two colours – pink and yellow, and divided by a thin layer of jam. She dropped us off with our cake which was so rich we couldn't finish it.

# Greer Baird 24-year-old passionate writer

The track was slowly disappearing with the fading light. My friend and I had been walking for what seemed like hours and, with night drawing on and the sun sinking below a green horizon, we became increasingly anxious to reach our destination.

Our current travels had started this morning, on arrival at 6am at Brisbane Airport, and with some eagerness we had headed out into unknown territory.

Jessie was the explorer and more adventurous than I was, always looking for darker, more dangerous paths that would lead to somewhere unknown and mysterious. Being lost was exciting to her and something of a challenge.

On the other hand I am the practical one, always getting out the old maps and marking our routes with a luminous yellow pen; camping trips on the South Downs, country road trips in Devon, walking up uneven gravelled lanes to small villages never visited before!

Beaming headlights emerged out of the darkness blurring my vision and, whilst I put my arm up to fend off the light from dazzling my eyes, a car pulled over in front of us. The driver must have thought I was flagging him down for a lift. Jessie jumped up with excitement and without hesitation skipped to the bonnet of the car and motioned me forward. I slowly walked over, at the same time looking at the ground and watching as the car's dipped headlights stroked the toes of my shoes.

Jessie had already hopped into the back seat but a sudden rush of anxiety engulfed my being and through half-squinted eyes the small dashboard light revealed a smiling figure. A young woman sat with her arms resting loosely over the steering wheel. I squashed in the back with Jessie, next to a pile of papers and banana skins. A sweet aroma filled the air and the radio emitted waves of country and western vocals with twangs so deep that they drowned out the rattling drone of the car's engine. The bangles on her wrist jangled as we drove along the bumpy road. She spoke of past journeys that she had taken which she longed for once more; she said that motherhood had shattered those dreams. And as she looked into the rearview mirror at our intrigued faces, she winked and said with a slight tremble in her voice, "Never give up on your dreams and always follow your heart, no matter where it takes you." We never did catch her name and as we pulled up outside our youth hostel, we knew that the moment was over, but there was a sparkle in her eyes, knowing that she had passed on a little bit of her life's history on to us. She waved goodbye as her rear lights were slowly swallowed up by the night's sky, never to be seen again...

To meet someone so inspiring on the first leg of our journey was more then we could have hoped for and it put us in high spirits, looking forward to who else might cross our paths on our travels. For us the ride had just begun but for her it was all over. Yet the memories she retained would stay with her forever.

## Jean-Jacques Lefevre carpenter

### 'Up the Workers'

Opportunities came – real practical ones. I got picked up by this character – very straight, very normal – he owned three or four furnishings shops, upmarket stuff, very expensive. I'd seen them, walked by them and could never have afforded anything in them. But we talked as equals, it seemed, and we got on. When I told him I was a joiner, he said he was opening this new shop in the 15th, and he said there was work for me there, how much did I charge? I made something up, hiked the price because I'd seen his shops and he said I had a start and he gave me the name of the foreman. And sure enough, I went along. It was a good run of work. He used to come around and see how it was going and I noticed he was friendly to me, but not like it was in the car; he reverted to type and so did I. Strange.

## 'HAN'

### 'Communication Short–Circuit'

You had to suffer some incredible bullshitting from drivers and I guess hitchers used to do it as well. So there you are, strangers unlikely to meet again. But drivers who gave me lifts used to set out on this huge bullshitting frenzy, fantasising not about sex necessarily, but how they had been in the SAS, or robbed banks or, as in the case of one guy, how he'd helped Lucan escape! I think in the end I met all this with a tired smile. Then you got people who were just loaded up with problems and wanted to talk. You did your best to help but most of the time you might just as well have not been there at all. And then people who would say nothing at all and out of politeness you'd try and make conversation, but some of them would not respond. Then you'd think, why the fuck did you pick me up? But then sometimes it was forced – when I hitched abroad, the language barrier seemed to bring people closer together. Great efforts were made by gesticulation or drawing pictures or anything to facilitate communication. I had a great laugh with a lot of people and, inevitably, some monumental communication breakdowns occurred which resulted in my ending up in the wrong place. I never had the heart to show my disappointment since they were so pleased that, in spite of the language barrier, we had apparently achieved our objective of understanding one another. So they went on in life, I guess, thinking that language doesn't matter. They concluded: "I picked up this English lad and I got him to where he wanted to go." Perhaps I should try and find that old Turk and put him right. Perhaps not – he would be disappointed with the truth.

# Alex Sebley photographer and artist

I was waiting on the edge of the main road onto Hayling Island with a female friend of mine at about 2 o'clock in the morning, desperate for a lift but not really considering that anyone might actually pick us up, as it was a such a late hour. But then, within a minute, a car pulled up and picked us up. It was a small car with 'surveillance' written on the side of it. The driver, a rotund, sunburned man with little hair, ushered us in and we gratefully entered the car. As we drove he spoke to us in a friendly manner, describing his line of work as a freelance surveillance operative. He had a secret camera installed in the front of his car and a couple of suitcases which looked like they carried heavy-duty equipment. He told us that he spent all his time filming the general public without having to leave his car, he just pointed the car at whatever or whoever he wished to film and the job was done. The footage was then used by lawyers as evidence in legal disputes and law enforcement. I thought that his job was crazy and imagined these scenarios of him making films all night, getting a strange voyeuristic kick out of it. I think he said something along the lines of, "You won't believe some of the women I've seen and what they get up to." Even though he was perfectly amiable I couldn't help but think there was some dark undertone to him.

# Julie MacDonald world traveller

After being holed up for a week in Rotorua with a bad back, it was time for Shivvy and I to move on. It was fortunate for me that my slipped disc had happened in the lap of luxury whilst staying with a friend's parents – the only problem being that I was still a smoker then and my friend's parents' house was strictly non-smoking. Consequently I had to haul myself out of bed and drag myself on to their front porch in the middle of a New Zealand winter just to have a cigarette!

Julie (our friend) drove us to the bus station on our departure, as there was a direct bus to Auckland several times a day – all we had to do was to 'phone Shivvy's cousin to let her know when we would be descending on them. This was again very fortunate as we were completely skint and had at least another three months to go before our trip was planned to end. This was why we were headed to Auckland, then into cheaper south east Asia.

We decided, despite my still fairly fragile back, to step our adventure up a gear and hitch. We saw no problem with this as we had been met by nothing but the utmost welcoming hospitality in New Zealand and we were not to be proved wrong.

I can't exactly remember how long we had been thumbing it when a nice-looking car containing, I have to say, a rather nice-looking man, stopped. He was going about half way to Auckland to a small town near Hamilton and after our experience of previous hitching journeys this was quite a good distance. During the journey, myself being the mouthy one with the bad back sat in the front, Shivvy quietly observant in the back, we discovered that our ride was Dutch. He was a sales rep, had been living in NZ for a few years and was absolutely mad on diving – the 'free fall' kind of diving without scuba gear. In fact, he was in the middle of patenting his 'big flipper' – one single flipper that both feet go into rather than the standard two separate ones which apparently gave much better manoeuvrability in the water. His favourite film was *The Big Blue* and I remember he spent quite a long time advocating why we should watch it!

By this stage it was quite late in the afternoon and there wasn't much daylight left. Adventurous though we were, we weren't quite stupid enough to hitch in the dark. We asked our kind chauffeur if he could drop us at the local bus station. He advised that there were no further buses to Auckland that day, and that he would be more than happy to put us up for the night and drop us at the station in the morning! Personally I think it was just a sad attempt on his part to ensure he gained another two recruits in to the 'I've watched *The Big Blue* club' as he had it on video.

He was actually due to be out that evening. He was coach to a youth diving group who had a competition some distance away. He was going to leave us to his food, his video, his bed and his ex-girlfriend (who he was obviously still on very good terms with). She had heard about my back and offered to take me to a natural hot spring complex nearby – which, in itself, was a bit bizarre as I sat in a hot bubbling pool outside in the dark with an air temperature of less that ten degrees celsius.

In the end our host's competition was cancelled and he ended up being home that evening, so he joined us to watch *The Big Blue* for the 705th time. He gave us a running commentary. As he promised, he dropped us off at the bus station the following morning and off we toddled to Auckland for some more free hospitality at Shivvy's cousin's house. After everything though – the hospitality, the free lift, the free room and quite a bizarre day altogether – four and a half years later, I'm quite ashamed to admit that I can't even remember his name.

## Lionel Fanthorpe author, radio and TV broadcaster

As a teenager I hitch-hiked all over the place from Dereham in Norfolk to Blackpool, and from Dereham to Yarmouth where my wife Patricia and I had a part-time job cleaning out caravans between lets. My happiest memory is not so much of hitch-hiking, as of bike-hiking. It happened like this. My old Ariel 350cc developed an electrical fault at around midnight and I was pushing it wearily up a hill, as it was illegal to ride without lights. The rest of the bike was fine and I knew that I could resume riding home at daybreak. I was overtaken by a group of friendly, helpful workers from the nearby Laing's Construction camp. They were on their way back from the village pub, and enquired about the bike problem. One then said, "Murphy's home for the weekend. You can have his bed in our hut." I accepted with alacrity. They not only provided a warm bed but a good supper and a mug of coffee. At first light I was away again. That's the joy of what real helpfulness and community spirit can be like. Strangers become friends and helpers. I shall always remember those kind and hospitable Irishmen with much gratitude. If only the whole world could be like them.

## Arnold Wesker playwright/director

My most intense period of hitch-hiking was during eighteen months conscription in the RAF. Few would refuse to pick up a young man in uniform. It was on one such a journey – I can't remember which way I was going, to or from London, and there was silence in the car. I didn't know what to say, and the driver didn't know what to ask after: "Come far?" As we drove through built-up areas, I watched him change gear again and again till finally I said, "You'd think it would be possible to invent gears that change automatically as you increase or decrease speed."

"They've been invented," he smiled.

## Chris Mitchell Spike magazine
### 'My First Ever Hitch...'

...which wasn't in some faraway country, but getting from Brighton to the Sussex University campus outside town. As a skint philosophy student, I got a lift from an HGV driver who resembled Lemmy from Motörhead. Despite beginning the journey with the fear it was going to end in a pile of twisted metal and burnt rubber, I learnt a lot in the ensuing fifteen-minute conversation before he safely set me down outside the campus gates.

# Sarah Barrett artist and lecturer

We set off quite early to get from Lampeter in west Wales to Oxford. It was a Sunday and the going was very slow – lots of lifts, but a mile here and a couple of miles there and a lot of waiting around. By late afternoon we had only reached Ross-on-Wye, which was less than halfway. As we wandered through the town bemoaning our luck and pretty unhappy about our prospects of getting home before nightfall, we came across a touristy wishing well. As a measure of our desperation, we threw a couple of coins in and wished for better luck. We found a reasonable place to begin hitching again and about five minutes later a guy stopped in a Volvo and we got in. He asked us where we were going and when we said Oxford, he said he was going to Cambridge, so could take us all the way there.

We got on very well with him – he was a mature veterinary student returning to college after a weekend at home. He was a speedy driver, the car was comfortable and he was good company. As it grew dark, he insisted on taking us into Oxford instead of dropping us on the outskirts so he could carry on through to Cambridge without going through the city. In fact, he dropped us right outside our flat between the Iffley and Cowley roads. So, if you are in Ross-on-Wye and down on your luck...

# Tim Burke consultant editor of *Young People Now*

'Reading to Edinburgh'

For her degree show in 1982 an art student friend of mine mounted a production, the very first fully-staged version, of Pablo Picasso's wartime play *Desire Caught By the Tail*. Her pals formed the cast and my, weren't we all a bunch of swells. The only time the play had been heard before was at a reading in Paris by a cast which included the likes of Albert Camus. We modern-day existentialist heroes decided the people of the Edinburgh Festival had to see this work – and we had a budget of, ooh, at least £40. Hence it was make your own way to Edinburgh, and anyone who got there was guaranteed a part. Thumbing it seemed the sensible option. I allowed a day and a half from Reading to Edinburgh and that's just what it took. In those days it was just so easy. Truckers were best as they were the longest lifts. For the price of a bit of shouted conversation you could easily gain 100 miles. 2CVs and Renault 4s, the more battered the better, were the next best hope – low on comfort but a very high stoppability quotient and that was what mattered. I was 20 years old. I'd had foreign holidays, I'd worked in France, but of England I knew little. I had no idea it was so, well, long. Happenstance led me up the M6 side of the country, and soon after Manchester I literally started to feel dizzy – despite the evidence of maps I felt, like some credulous member of Columbus's crew, that I was at risk of dropping off the end of the world. But alongside this Southern ignorance was a youthful spirit of adventure that, seen from comfortable middle age, seems extraordinary. Stuck in the middle of Cumbria? Getting dark? Haven't seen a car for fifteen minutes? OK, I'll climb over this fence and put a tent up. In the morning I awoke to find a half-tonne of Friesian cow investigating the opening of my tent – now, I would be terrified; then, it was all part of the fun. I quickly progressed to the services on the M8, awaiting the final stage of my journey into the capital. I'm in luck – a Volvo estate pulls over, a quietly spoken chap gets out and helps me off with my backpack. Now here was room and comfort, and someone who showed a genuine interest in my Fringe adventure. Observing the etiquette of the situation, I counter with "And what do you do?" "I'm a member of the European Parliament," comes the not altogether expected reply. Not only that, he was chair of the Agriculture committee and had a meeting with Scottish and Newcastle Breweries at their venerable buildings at the bottom of the Royal Mile. Frankly I was intimidated – but that was the wonder of hitching. You met good people – you met politicians with a heart – you had your expectations confounded. As we arrived at the offices a uniformed flunky was guarding the gates and nervously surveying the roads for the arrival of their VIP. A gaggle of Suits stood by. I felt way out of my depth and was wondering how I could slink away quietly. We pulled into the tiny car park and I prepared to make myself scarce before I was surely chased out by hefty security guards. But my MEP would have none of it. Totally ignoring the increasingly jumpy S&N management, he helped me on with my rucksack, shook my hand and wished me all the best as he me waved off towards Canongate. By such small acts of kindness are our lives changed. I went away feeling important – more important for the moment than the boss of an FT 100 company. It was a practical lesson in human relations – whoever they are, be nice to people. You never know the impact that a little respect can have.

# Sergey Kharitich (St Petersburg, Russia), MA in Translation/Interpreting; practising hitch-hiking since 1998; editor-in-chief of www.hike.ru news portal since 2004.

## 'Russians on the Road: Give it a Try'

Hitch-hiking is a wonderful opportunity not only to save money while travelling but also to see many places without being dictated to by timetables, airports and railway stations. Hitch-hiking has always afforded me the opportunity to meet different people from different backgrounds with different viewpoints, and learn from their experiences.

In some five years of hitch-hiking, I have been picked up by hundreds of drivers. Drivers in Ladas and Mercedes, Porsches and Neoplan buses... Farmers, teachers, managing directors, students... Over a dozen countries, thousands of kilometres of roads varying from highways to dirt roads in the middle of nowhere. Everyone knows that you do not remember all the drivers that ever picked you up, especially after two dozen or so. However, some stay in your memory for a long time. Here is the story of one; in fact, it is two stories in one...

We were hitching back home from a long trip through Finland, Sweden, Norway, Denmark and northern Germany. After we got off the Puttgarden ferry at Rødby, Denmark, we were hitching just beyond the terminal with ferries arriving every 40-45 minutes and cars going out at a fairly low speed, which was good for hitch-hiking. It still proved difficult though, since the first lane was mostly occupied by trucks. We stood there for a couple of hours until an old Sierra with Danish number plates stopped a hundred metres behind us. The driver jumped out of the car and beckoned to us.

"Hi, how are you?"

"OK, fine!"

"Are you going to Copenhagen?"

"Yeah, to Copenhagen."

"Could you give us a lift to Karlslunde?" (I knew there was a good petrol station there, just before Copenhagen.)

"No problem, I can take you to Copenhagen if you like... Where do you come from?"

"From Russia, we're on our way home via Denmark, Sweden and Finland."

"You're Russians?"

"Yes, we are."

"Well, you know... I'm not really going to Copenhagen, so I can't really help you there..."

"But how far are you going? Maybe you can take us to Karlslunde?"

"Sorry, guys. I have to go, I'm in a hurry."

And off he went!

I know the reason why he decided to change his mind in just a couple of seconds. You may guess the reason, too. It was a very strange thing to experience in a country that claims to be democratic and open to other cultures and nationalities. I know that all Danes are not the same, and one should not consider one instance to be the rule. I had lived in Denmark for five months, seen and talked to many Danes and still consider some as good friends. I take people as people, be they Danes or Britons, Russians or Chinese, and believe this to be the only way we should treat each other. Why do we not appreciate that representatives of a nation are not all the same, just as our fingers are not all the same?

Another hitching experience which took place a couple of weeks earlier in the north of Sweden further illustrates my point. We were crossing Sweden from Luleå to Kiruna to go on to Narvik in Norway, when a grey Volvo pulled up with an Egyptian driving and two young girls in the back.

"Hi! Are you going somewhere in the direction of Kiruna?"

"Well yeah, that way... Where do you want to go?"

"All the way to Narvik and then south to Oslo."

"I can take you as far as Gällivare, if you like..."

"That'll be great, thanks!"

We got in and started chatting with the driver. Some ten or fifteen minutes later he asked where we came from. When he learned we were from Russia, he got more excited and interested and started asking more questions. He also told us about himself: he had moved to Sweden from Egypt several years ago and worked as an engineer, got married, had two lovely daughters, got divorced... We continued talking about the weather, the Swedes, the mountains, about family and countries...

"Did you say you're going to Narvik?" he asked us.

"Yeah, that's right," we replied.

"I can take you on to Kiruna, since I'm not really going to Gällivare, but to a village a couple of miles further down the road. Is that OK with you?"

"Well, it'll be better if you drop us off at the turning to Kiruna – it'll be easier for us to get a lift there than in the village..."

"OK, I'll drop you off there!"

We talked and talked, and stopped for a while for the driver to get some rest, then continued talking. He told us there were plenty of Russians in the area, some of them making real trouble – he told us about two Russians who hired a cab and killed the driver – this made us feel uncomfortable and ashamed of some of our compatriots.

We were just about to reach the turning when, suddenly, he said, "I can take you all the way to Kiruna if you like?"

"That's nice of you, but do you have time for that?"

"I am going to Kiruna anyway, so it won't be a problem."

"But you said..."

"Well, you know... You don't speak Swedish and you're not from here, so I wanted to find out what kind of people you were and what you were up to. When you said you're from Russia, frankly, I was reluctant to take you any further than Gällivare – you know all these stories with ex-USSR people. And I have two young daughters in the car... However, we have a saying in Egypt: people are not the same, just as fingers are not the same. And we know that Swedes can also be troublemakers. I'm now sure you have nothing to do with those murderers and I'm glad I didn't drop you off earlier and that I've helped you out a bit more." He added, "You seem very nice people to talk to! I am travelling further down to Narvik tomorrow morning to take my daughters for a picnic, so I could take you a bit further if you don't get an earlier lift."

It was getting dark, and night was coming on, so the offer was sensible enough. But luckily, we were to get a lift almost to the Norwegian border some thirty minutes later.

"Hope we find a lift before morning," we said to him. "And thanks for the offer. Maybe we'll see you tomorrow!"

"Good luck, take care."

At first we had strange feelings about that man, but he was just being careful. Maybe a bit too careful, but then considering his daughters had spent several hours in the same car as complete strangers, I couldn't blame him. Who knows how I might act in the same situation? Would I be immediately judgmental or would I try to get to know the person I had picked up? Who knows?

Of course, it is perhaps not very pleasant to be tested and approved 'before use' just because of your nationality, but the approach of the

Egyptian seemed more logical and constructive than that of the Dane.

If you are still afraid of Russians roaming the roads of a 'civilized' Europe, I am sure if you 'test' us, you will like us. When you drop us off you will say, "See you again on the road!" If you pick up another Russian hitch-hiker later you will ask him "Are you Russian? I picked up two great Russians! I picked them up last summer/winter/spring/autumn in Sweden/Belgium/Scotland/etc." instead of asking the usual stereotypical questions like "Do you have snow all year round?" or "Is it true that bears roam the streets in your towns?" which, strange as it may seem, some people still ask.

Just because you don't know us is no reason not to get to know us. Just make this small step towards us and you will see we are normal people. And you will never regret it.

## David Nelson  Deputy Chairman, Foster and Partners architects

I tried it twice! The first time I was penniless, attempting to get from Loughborough to London for reasons I cannot remember. I like to think it was to meet a lady but... Anyway, I walked out to the spur road and stood there all day... no lift... maybe my 1969 shoulder-length hair had something to do with it.

The second time I was a bit drunk and 100 yards from home – thumb out, instant lift! Thereafter my only hitch-hiking successes were courtesy of someone else's thumb.

## Nigel Billen  editor ACE Tennis magazine

My hitch-hiking experience is limited to cadging lifts. But it's amazing how friendly people can be. For some reason, one cold winter's day about ten years ago while holidaying in the Catskills, New York, my girlfriend and I thought it might be culturally enlightening to witness a Passing Out parade at West Point, the military academy. A bus handily took us there and we enjoyed our snoop at the clean-cut young cadets on their proudest day. What we hadn't reckoned on was the absence of a bus back to the hotel we were staying in. America may be the land of the car and the entrepreneur, but that doesn't mean outside the big cities, you will find a cab. The only thing to do was ask one of the sets of proud parents if they might be going our way. The very first we asked said yes and we bundled into an over-sized Ford along with extended family.

Just meeting them was an insight into US life. Our driver's only disappointment seemed to be that he didn't have to travel further out of his way to deliver us safely back to our hotel.

# Max Arthur author

In 1959 I had been in the RAF just a few months when I learned I had a fortnight's leave. I was still in touch with some school mates back home in Bognor Regis, and on the basis of many hours successfully hitching in uniform, dreamed up the bright idea of thumbing a lift with two of them – Dennis and Alan – all the way from Bognor to a campsite at La Ciotat, just outside Marseilles.

We received our brand new passports from Little Venice and our ill-prepared expedition set out. All went well as far as Dieppe. But for some reason there our luck ran out. People in cars looked askance at us, clearly wanting nothing to do with three crew-cut thugs with enormous rucksacks, and quickly accelerated past. Eventually, a middle-aged lady, who must have worked in the wartime Resistance to have the courage to pick us up, drove us to the motorway. When she pulled up the handbrake of her 2CV, it came away in her hand! We mumbled Vive la France, shook her hand and smiled guilt-ridden smiles. It was not a great start.

Still, there was the signpost to Marseilles, telling us it was only 1,000 kilometres away. Dennis, the clever one, worked that out to be 627 miles. Our optimism didn't last long, however, as lorry, car, lorry, car, lorry, lorry, car – and more bloody cars and lorries – drove past without giving us a glance. By now, I was ranting. 'We bloody bailed you out in 1944, didn't we? If it wasn't for our fathers, you bastards would be under the yoke of the Nazis.' My own father's war experience had not seriously disturbed Hitler's sleep, so I'm not sure where all this rage came from.

We decided that three ruffians together were never going to get a lift, and so we would split up and make our own way to La Ciotat. Dennis gave me a phrase in French that I was to say to any driver who stopped. One or two did, but when I muttered the phrase, 'Ou est Marseilles?' the look on their faces clearly said, 'Who is this dickhead?' I was turning out to be a lost character in a Samuel Beckett play in which I was struggling doggedly with beginnings, and especially, as it was working out, with endings. My journey was now representing a perception of meaninglessness and total incoherence. Beckett would have understood – but he wasn't there. He was tucked away in Paris, enjoying his success.

All I found at that moment of existential crisis was Harold, standing forlornly by the roadside. Harold was straight out of *Waiting For Godot*. Not only for him was Godot not going to appear, but neither was any motorist going to stop. There was an intrinsic sadness to Harold. It was as if life had passed him by. As we stood together on the side of the road, he said in a dull voice, 'I'm getting a boat from Marseilles'. 'Oh,' I replied, 'I'm going that way too.' And so for the next three days we slowly made our way south together, spending one night wrapped in plastic sheeting and lying in a ditch.

For the last 300 miles we travelled, if that is the word for it, in the back of a gigantic empty lorry with a small window on the roof. We had no idea where the driver was going. Out of desperation, we'd simply climbed into the back and he'd locked us in. Harold became upset at me asking whether the white-slave-trade embraced young men. We were thrown around in the back for miles, all the time thinking we'd end up as sliced salami in Tangier if we didn't give up our bodies. Then, after what seemed like days, the lorry stopped. We waited to be let out. We banged on the door – but no one came. After hours of this, the very drunk driver let us out. He'd obviously got pissed, and then, in the one remaining fragment of his brain that was sober, remembered us. I pumped his hand as you do a prison warden who tells you your execution has been delayed.

'I don't know about you, Max, but that was a bit frightening,' Harold said. 'It was, Harold. It was.' By now I had grown quite fond of Harold. A glass of cheap red wine and a jambon sarnie at a local café and we were ready for the Côte d'Azur, thirty miles away. It was getting dark and Harold suggested we stay at a pension – but I persuaded him that we should push on. So we were pretty weary when a French soldier dropped us off on the bleak outskirts of Marseilles at 3am. We walked down dingy, unlit streets, hoping to find somewhere to put our heads for the remainder of the night. I'd look round and Harold was trudging lugubriously behind, not encouraged by remarks like, 'Must be something along here.' There wasn't. It was growing colder, so I thought we might as well sleep in a doorway. 'This will do, Harold,' I said, looking at a covered porch and taking off my rucksack. No reply came from Harold – but I'd got used to his silences. Then I looked up – and Harold wasn't there. 'He's probably gone for a pee in one of the ruined houses,' I thought. But after a few minutes he still hadn't reappeared. 'Harold, where are you?' No reply. I didn't want the local people opening their shutters and bawling at me in the street, so I was whispering his name as loud as I could. But no Harold came. There was no sign of him – he'd simply disappeared into the night.

My new friend, whom I had grown fond of, and whose surname I had never learned, nor address taken, had gone. Had gone forever. Nearly 50 years on, his doleful face still haunts me.

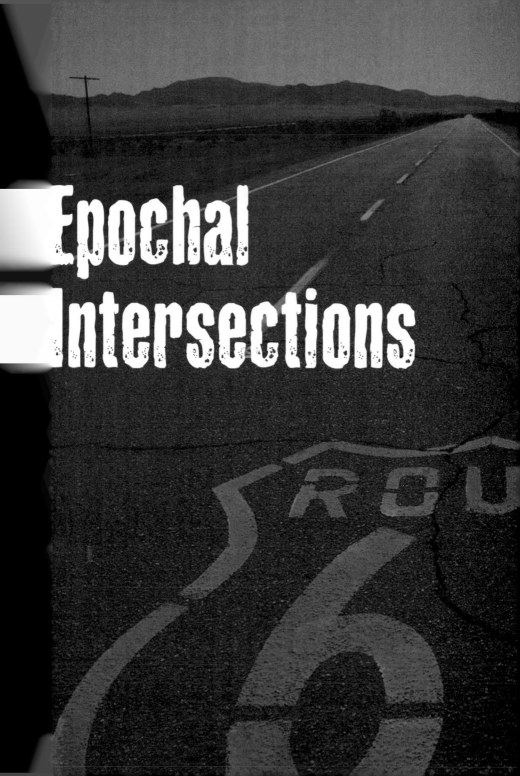

# Epochal
# Intersections

# Eric Burdon

"performing artist, traveller, dreamer, sometimes referred to as 'rock star'."

## 'Thumbs Up' (with J. Marshall Craig)

My true christening came when I was in college – I was 16 going on 17 and enduring the first few awkward, pimply months of Newcastle College of Art & Industrial Design. It was there that this once-innocent and naive Geordie lad was introduced to jazz, blues and R&B, a definitively shakubuku moment that change my life forever.

I treasured nearly every LP I could get my paws on but fate led me down a remarkable road during a trip to London. Uncharacteristically, I didn't hitch-hike but instead took my Dad's old Italian scooter – a hellish trip that from the start I regretted taking in quite the manner that I did.

But once in London, my turmoil along the tarmac and dusty roads evaporated in the glow of the great musical wonders that waited to be discovered. Among them was a copy of a jazz magazine called, simply, *Jazz Monthly*, that was handed to me by a nice stranger in the Dobells record store. The stranger was Alexis Korner – soon to be a lifelong friend and the godfather, if you will, of bringing the American blues to England and being, ultimately, responsible for everything from The Beatles to the Rolling Stones, The Yardbirds, The Who, Long John Baldry, Graham Bond and, in no small way, a Newcastle band called The Animals – the first British band to knock The Beatles off the top of the charts, with 'House of the Rising Sun'.

I remember so clearly reading that magazine that Alexis handed me. From cover to cover and again, hoping each retracing would enlighten me to something I'd missed. And on one of these deep studies I notice an advertisement in the back announcing a festival planned for Antibes in the south of France, featuring the great Ray Charles.

Brother Ray! My art classes had even taken a back seat to my living in the world and what I had heard being conjured from the vinyl grooves of *Live in Atlanta*, a Ray Charles LP that I'd bought and made a nightly ritual of listening to. I knew every phrase, every nuance – every breath that the microphones had captured of Ray on that record. When I saw the ad that he was going to be in France, it was like my quest for Mecca that I be there and see him perform.

First thought: Dump the scooter. The way to Ray was thumbs-up from Newcastle to the pastoral southern French climes. Not that this was an arbitrary whim – Kerouac's cross-America chronicle *On the Road* had been, since its 1957 publication, a universal bohemian odyssey that influenced writers, readers and even the enemy of the American establishment; more immediate and more personally, it had become my personal bible, alternatively promising and warning of the questionable gifts of Western culture.

As such, I'd created the mobile Eric Burdon infantry: A sleeping bag with a piss hole sewn in the middle, wrapped around a survival pack of canned baked beans, Swiss Army knife and US military rain poncho.

It was a kit I'd put to good use in the past – mostly to the rage of my parents. We'd previously been on vacation in Europe, which meant I had a passport at an early age, and I'd struck out on my own for Paris out of sheer, blinding curiosity and to the horror and admonishment of my parents. So I kept my plans a secret. None of my running buddies was up for the trek, so it was truly Eric embracing the world alone for the most righteous reason imaginable: American gospel/blues music.

While a lot of my life since the meteoric success of the original Animals has blown by in a confusing gumbo of images, there are a few instances where I retain total, unimpeachable clarity. And this was one of them. I remember that Ray was playing on August 14th in France. So there I was in the first week of the month, my bindle at my feet just outside of Gateshead with a smile on my face and the promise of Brother Ray in my heart … and the thick gritty diesel exhaust of the passing trucks in my lungs. My tenaciousness was soon rewarded when a Glaswegian trucker swung his Leyland on to the shoulder for me.

"OK, laddie," he said, his paw-like hands on the wheel and the shifter and a smile on his ruddy whisky-veteran face. "Where ya off te?"

"Well," I answered, "the south of France, actually."

"Oh, deary me," he answered teasingly in a mock light-in-the-loafers English accent. "Well, I'm to Middlesbrough … you'll have te walk the rest o' the way."

"No way, man," I said. "I'm lucky with me thumb."

He had of course caught my Newcastle accent immediately but had waited to comment. "Geordie, are ya?"

"Why, aye, man," I said, turning up my hometown dialect. He responded in kind.

"What takes a lad like thee off te the south o' France? Coulda be one o' those Frenchie girls?"

I was still young enough to blush – and old enough to fantasize – and I thought almost instantly of Bardot in *And God Created Woman*.

"No," I answered, "but ah might fine one ya know!"

The trucker laughed out loud. "Well, if ya lose yer bottle ye can make it back te Geordie land tomorrow." He looked and me and winked. "So if it's no a girlie, what is it then, if ya don't mind me askin'?"

"Music," I said, loudly and proudly.

"Must be sometin' to go all that way."

I waited a little while and then said, "A black man – a blind black man from America."

"Aye, those darkies do have a way wit music and dance."

I had a flash temper in my youth and in an instant my gratitude for the ride turned into a barely contained desire to punch this jerk's lights out. Believe me, I'm no 21st-century Sensitive Man – but from the time I could walk and talk I had zero tolerance for racism of any kind. Part of this came from the good teachings of my parents and part from having been born literally as the genocidal Nazis were dropping their bombs on my hometown. So I was nothing but relieved when Middlesbrough appeared and I found welcome relief from this bastard by jumping out at the first roundabout.

It was late in the day and getting cold – I was hungry and not too confident I'd get another ride to London, so I started planning to spend the night at a garage or truckers' stop. So I started walking. Of course, if you're hitchin' it's your face drivers want to see, not your arse – but I didn't care. I knew that I just had to make London, where I knew I could call Alexis Korner and find refuge.

A few cars passed by, ignoring my extended thumb. Then an Austin Healey 3000 ripped past. I thought I saw his brake lights flash far down the road but my hope was short-lived. There was traffic on the northbound lane, which did me no good – or so I thought. I glanced over and saw the Austin coming from the south and the driver taking a good look at me. He'd pulled a U-turn and then pulled another and stopped right in front of me.

"Come on then," he said. "Put yer bag in the back. And fasten yer seatbelt."

I'd never seen a seatbelt before.

"Put yer legs straight and hold on tight," the driver said, slamming into first gear and taking off like a rocket. He picked me up, he said, to balance the weight of the car, which he was planning on racing in Bradford. This offered him opportunity for a little practice amongst the light traffic on the slightly wet tarmac. I was nothing but game!

"You all right?" he yelled as we tore down the highway.

"Oh yeah! Fuckin' great!"

I'd never made time like this hitching before! Unfortunately, he wasn't going all the way to London and dropped me just outside of Grantham. Must have been around 10 pm. I knew I wasn't likely to get a ride and started thinking about finding a place to tuck myself in for the night. At least I had the thought of Brigitte's pouting mouth keeping me warm inside as Brother Ray's voice bounced around my brain.

A Jaguar passed by. Jags never stopped.

I kept walking and saw a brick wall. Someone's garden, partially sheltered by a glass covering. Shelter – at least the best I was going to find that night. I unrolled my bindle and snuggled up and was soon asleep. For how long I don't know – as I was rather shockingly awoken by a bright flashlight in my face behind which was the unmistakable voice of a constable. I tried to explain myself but the cop interrupted me. "Well lad, it's like this: People don't take to strangers sleeping in their vegetable sheds."

I guess I'd made too much noise getting over the wall and settling in and had alarmed the homeowners.

The constable lowered his torch and his serious tone. He said that if I promised to disappear before sun-up he'd leave me be. I promised.

"Okay then, laddie. Good luck."

My luck was good!

The next day, I soon caught a southbound truck and found myself in North London near a tube station and a telephone box.

"Where are ya?" asked the gravelly voice of Alexis on the other end of the phone.

"Hampstead," I answered.

"Well, come on, man – the pipe is burning and the tea's hot!"

It wasn't hard to remember where Alexis lived. Moscow Road. At one end the elaborate Greek Orthodox Church and at the other end the Soviet Embassy. What a cool place to live!

When I arrived he greeted me like he always did: "Hello, Eric Victor Burdon!" He pointed at my shoes. "Leave 'em at the door." And he waved me warmly into the flat.

This was the man who sparked the entire British blues movement ... his place was warmed by a small electric heater in the middle of the room. Posters lined the walls above the stacks of books, LPs, tapes and magazines. Candles were ablaze seemingly in every spare inch of space in the room. Alexis brought me some fresh coffee, lit some incense and handed me a well-packed hash pipe. I had never been so comfortable in my life!

We spent the day and evening listening to music that blew my mind, and talking about everything under the sun. Alexis was so impressed that I was on a loner mission to see Ray Charles. I drifted off and had probably the best sleep I've ever had and slept until noon. Then I caught the ferry to France. From heaven to utter hell: the crossing was, as it usually is, nothing short of torture. I couldn't speak French, but I sure could throw up in French!

I changed my money at the port and stuffed 400 francs in my socks. Nearly immediately after throwing my thumb skyward, I was picked up by a trucker in a big blue rig. He was soon disappointed to learn we had no common language, but was generous. I returned the favour and bought him lunch at one of the gas stops. Unlike England – or anywhere else in the world – even the gas stop food was good in France and there was a very decent wine that came with the inexpensive meal.

My luck the following day was not as fortuitous. I went without a single ride and spent the night in a wooden bus shelter.

The next morning a truck stopped for me and I continued on my way toward Bordeaux. It was hot and dusty and the cab was like a sauna with diesel incense.

By the time we stopped, I realized that I'd gone off my direct path – and I wasn't actually sure what day it was, either. If I could only see the water, I figured, I'd feel a lot better about where I was.

The trucks were getting scarcer, and I ended up spending one day walking, taking a break only during the midday hours when it was hottest. That night I was getting a little desperate again and, when I saw a gendarme office, I knocked on the door. The cop didn't need to speak English to know that I was lost and in distress but he was a complete prick and refused to help me or offer me shelter. I spent the night on a wooden bench in the waiting room of a train station, having eaten my last can of beans cold. At some point during the night car lights woke me and even before I could rouse myself from the hard bench a man entered.

"Toilette?" he asked.

"Yes, yes," I said, and pointed.

His car was pointed west – the direction I needed to go, so I was hopeful. The guy came out of the toilet still pulling up his fly and walked past me quickly, ignoring everything I said.

"Sir, please! I need a ride! Hey, come on! I need your help!"

He kept walking straight to his car and jumped in and slammed the door without so much as a glance at me. So I ran out in front of his car to stop him. That's the only time we had eye contact – and it was clear that he wasn't going to stop. I had to jump out of the way because the bastard really would have run me down.

My right elbow took the brunt of my fall and hurt like hell, though even as I screamed out in pain and anger I knew there wasn't a soul within earshot.

The next morning I headed out again on the road west. And then, a vision! A Land Rover covered in camping gear and – most importantly – British plates!

I turned to face them as they approached and they smiled as they pulled over. They were a married couple on holiday and waved me over. I so happily joined them, tossing my bindle up onto the already packed roof. After pleasant introductions and small talk they were quite interested to hear of my trek and all I'd been through to see Ray Charles. I remember telling them that I was a singer in a band myself and hoped to some day go pro.

They told me they couldn't take me all the way to Antibes, but that they could take me to the coast and I could venture north from there. They also told me that Pablo

Picasso had a beach house along the way, and to keep an eye out for him since he was often in the local cafés and restaurants and loved the water.

My luck had indeed turned around for the better. I soon found myself walking up the beach, my boots tied together and hanging around my neck. In the distance, I saw a single person a mile or two away. As I approached, there was no doubt as to his identity: it was Picasso!

The tide had been out and was slowly coming back in. The great artist had been drawing an elaborate design in the wet sand with a sharp stick; it was obviously a deeply personal moment and I was reluctant to approach. Then again, I couldn't keep away! I was sole witness to this magic. The tide was returning quickly and Pablo scrawled his signature in the sand as I approached and fumbled for my Dad's camera. I advanced the film and lifted the viewfinder to my eye just as Picasso noticed me and turned. All I could see was an angry glare. I lowered the camera to try to explain myself as the sea washed into his creation. I lifted the camera again, since I knew this was the last moment this piece of art – and certainly my opportunity to capture it – would exist. I pushed the button and there was a half click. It was the end of the roll. One more wave washed in and there was nothing left of Picasso's creation. He stormed off and all that was left were the footprints of a genius.

By the time I got to Antibes I discovered that I was one day too late to see Ray Charles. He had moved on to Rome. I had nothing to do but return to Paris and then home.

Over the years, I told friends and newspaper reporters this story as a way of explaining how important the American blues music I heard was to me as a teenager.

It had been so long that, actually, I'd sort of forgotten about it. Until just a year ago, when I was in Las Vegas to catch a Paul McCartney show. I popped backstage to say hello and was talking to a few friends when Sir Paul snuck up behind me and stuck a finger in the middle of my back and whispered in my ear: "Eric's gone ... lookin' for Ray Charles!"

# Alastair Campbell
## 'The Day Jacques Brel Died'

As part of my university education, I spent a year in France teaching English
at a school in Nice. During my spare time, 1 busked around Europe with my
bagpipes. One day I was hitching from Aix-en-Provence back to Nice, and was
picked up by a Belgian lorry driver. During the journey there was a news
flash that the singer Jacques Brel had died, and the lorry driver, this great
hulking bloke, burst into tears. The radio station then played back-to-back
Brel songs for the whole journey. I've been hooked on Brel ever since.

# James Hobbs journalist

I once unwittingly hitch-hiked into history. In November 1990 I was going from a flat
in Bristol – a satisfyingly short walk from the slip road to the M32 with a steady supply
of traffic and no immediate competition – to visit friends in London. A lorry driver
stopped to pick me up, dropping me, rather surprisingly, I thought, considering he was
delivering a load of bedroom furniture, outside the Tate Gallery at Millbank. For weeks
the news had been full of the leadership struggle within the Conservative party.
I walked up to Downing Street in time to see Margaret Thatcher returning in the back
of a Jaguar from a trip to Paris, convinced still, at that time, that she could keep her
grip on the leadership.

I still like to think that my own rather feeble call of "Resign!" as she disappeared
towards the door of No. 10 that evening played some small part in her overnight
decision to stand down as prime minister. Strangely, though, the end of Thatcher
heralded the beginning of the end of hitch-hiking for me. As she left her job, so my
chances of getting employment increased, and I could afford public transport. My last
great hitch was a month spent travelling around Ireland with the woman I married.

Now we live in London and bikes and buses are the only way to travel, although
once I hitch-hiked across the city with spectacular success, and I am sure it should be
encouraged as a way to get around the capital. Our car's back seats are now cluttered
with child seats and toys. Even if there still were hitch-hikers, it would be difficult to fit
them in.

# Patrik Swerner

One morning in the Swiss mountains I got a lift from two elderly Spanish people. One of them was an artist, a famous artist. He looked crestfallen like a child when we had to admit that we'd not heard of him. Art to me in those days was the nearest and loudest rock 'n' roll so it wasn't surprising I'd not heard of Salvador Dali. Was it really Salvador Dali? I don't recall a funny moustache. Anyway, they dropped us off at Lucerne.

# Sam Andrew writer, artist and the guitarist who played the most nights with Janis Joplin of any musician in her life. Now Sam paints, sculpts and plays jazz piano when he is not on the road with Big Brother and the Holding Company

It was a beautiful July in 1966 and Big Brother and the Holding Company were going to Vancouver, British Columbia, to play at The Pacific National Exhibition Gardens Auditorium. This was our first trip outside the US and each of us was excited. Janis Joplin saw this trip as another station on her way to becoming a star. Peter Albin, Big Brother's eternal tour guide and social activities director, was eager to visit all of the tourist attractions. James Gurley and I were looking forward to meeting some Canadian musicians and hearing their experiences in this new counterculture scene. These are some of the things that we thought would happen on this Vancouver trip.

Here are some things that actually did happen. We slept on the floor in a store front room. Janis and I unknowingly drank a beverage that had LSD in it and so we stayed up all night on a beach in West Vancouver with a full moon shining down talking about God and the Universe. The next morning the entire band was thrown out of The Jolly Roger restaurant and all we wanted was breakfast. I suppose they didn't like the way we looked. Or smelled. Patchouli oil was the perfume of choice in the band.

Oh, yes, and right at the beginning of the entire trip, the person who was supposed to pick us up at Seattle airport was a no-show. We were stuck with all of our equipment and all of our baggage. Fortunately the amplifiers were on wheels. We put our suitcases and guitars on top and rolled everything out to the freeway and HITCH-HIKED TO VANCOUVER with all of our gear. I would not believe this if it had not actually happened to me. Oddly enough, I cannot remember who picked us up. What freeway angel would have the courage and generosity to haul hairy strangers to the mellow North? Blessings on her/him, blessings and benedictions. Amen.

# Bernd Wechner committed hitch-hiker and columnist for Suite101.com

## 'The International Hitch-Hiking Conference'

I first heard about the International Hitch-Hiking Conference (IHHC) in 1998. It was the second such conference to take place. For the third conference, I made the extraordinary trip from my home in Geneva to Vilnius, Lithuania to take part myself. I hitched some two thousand kilometres in thirty-four hours. I had to hitch – what option was there? It was, after all, a hitch-hiking conference.

For the fourth conference in the year 2000 I wasn't so keen. Frankly, to hitch 2000 kilometres and back takes a lot of energy and enthusiasm – easy to muster the first time, when it's a fresh adventure. But this time, I was busy at home, and low on energy and enthusiasm. However, I did want to visit the Conference and catch up with the lovely folk it draws. A dilemma of sorts. An internal voice prohibited a plane or train. Just not good form, by Jove! So basically I called the whole thing off.

Then a friend of mine, Louise, confided that she was depressed, and had cancelled a trip to Prague. She'd taken up hitching six months earlier, in no small part due to my corrupting influence. She'd grown to love it as a friendly, reliable, cheap way of getting around Switzerland. I figured an adventure in good company might cheer her up and suggested that if she wanted to, I'd be prepared to hitch to the Conference with her.

At the last minute she agreed. I was nervous and unsure. Not only was this a crazy venture, but now I had the self-imposed responsibility of bringing someone else all that way and back again in time for work.

We left Thursday morning and all went fine as far as Berlin, where we arrived at about 2 am on the Friday morning. We crashed at my ex's place, conveniently situated in the south-eastern corner of the Berlin ring-road.

That morning she took us to the Polish border where, unfortunately, because Louise had no visa, she was refused entry. She would have to go back to Berlin to get a visa, and we had no time for this!

Torn between options, it was decided that she would simply return home and I would carry on. I got a lift right the way to Marijampole, Lithuania from the border and was invited home by Romus, whose lovely wife Loretta had prepared the national speciality, Zeppelins, for breakfast.

I set out for Vilnius later that morning and arrived among crowds of familiar faces and warm embraces. Two friends of mine, Robert Prins and Skot Rogers, were there, making it a record as far as Western attendance was concerned. Some eighty people were present, whereas normally there would have been only fifty or so.

The Conference itself took place in the Municipal Hall, decked out like a parliamentary chamber. It was far too large and formal for the nature of the event, but still a warm gesture from the town to offer it free of charge to us. It was free-form as usual, with a vague agenda, timetable, even a printed programme, but in all honesty, the talks and events all come second to simple gossip and networking. Much like any conference, really!

On both Saturday and Sunday nights there was plenty of beer and food, and very little sleep. Only in Lithuania can you buy a beer with a coin, and get a note in return! For some reason there are 5 Litas coins and 1 Litas notes in circulation. There were videos playing, some fringe meetings, a talk or two as well as an excursion around town, and the Kaziuko Muge, a unique craft fair in the streets of Vilnius which takes place only once a year and draws in Lithuanians from across the country.

Aside from the formal story-telling forum, many stories circulate outside of the programme. A certain sense of stage fright dominates, which beer serves to alleviate. "It's a small world" stories are not uncommon and well-loved. I recall my friend Dimitri's story. He was hitching through Poland when he recognised a manager from his job at Latvian Telecom driving by. They exchanged a wave, but the manager's car was full up with five people and luggage; so no room for Dimitri. However, when he got back home he received an email from the manager and got a promotion and healthy pay rise out of it!

I missed many of the beautiful Russians I remembered from the previous year. Admittedly we had little language in common, but nonetheless I regretted not seeing these vibrant faces and characters again, simply because Russians need visas and invitations to enter Lithuania, unless they sneak across the border in the middle of the night, which requires a lot of energy and planning. I could well understand them not coming this year. It's only thanks to Louise that I made it.

The trip back was mean. Real mean. I had a 1.5 metre stalk of dried flowers from the market to take along, and it took forever to get home. On Monday morning, I was accompanied to the border by Wenda and Petr, two Czechs headed the same way.

You won't believe it, but the three of us thumbing together made better time than Tomek, Asia and Michal, three Poles who took the bus to the border that same morning!

From there it went downhill. There was no border traffic and I entered Poland with a through ride. I arrived in Berlin sleepless about 7 am on Tuesday morning, having hitched all night through Poland, mostly on trucks. I'd received two invitations to spend the night and move on in the morning, which I declined. Tonight, however, there were not many rides. I was 8 hours behind schedule with no time to sleep. I showered, ate, collected Louise and got going again.

Things didn't improve. We got stuck in two or three spots costing us time we no longer had. We stood for an hour at Schauinsland services around midnight with no traffic to speak of. Then a car with Vaudoise plates pulled up. Not only was this car from right near Geneva, but it was an old friend of mine from Lausanne, Celestine. She kindly took us to the border but wasn't crossing until the next day.

We got another ride soon enough to the other side of Basel, where we got stuck again. Some friendly police wished us luck and a couple of service station attendants invited us in from the cold, but we kept hitching in spite of the lack of cars.

Eventually we were saved at 2 am by Daniel, a gracious Belgian headed for Mont Blanc to go hang-gliding. He pulled over, intending to sleep, but we twisted his arm ever so gently and he agreed to continue driving on to Geneva. We arrived around 6 am after thirty-six hours non-stop hitching, I had to be at work at 8:30 ... needless to say I was late.

# Philip Conford historian

"Was heading for Bristol, but a bloke offered me a lift to Yorkshire, so I took it." This sentence from my diary for Sunday October 9th 1966 encapsulates the sheer random excitement of my own personal response to Jack Kerouac's *On the Road*: a 30-hour hitch-hiking binge which I undertook about three weeks after my 18th birthday. But why had I been heading for Bristol? The diary doesn't record my motives, and after nearly four decades I haven't the faintest notion. I do remember, though, that with all the heartless lack of imagination of the typical teenager I gave no thought to how my disappearance westwards or northwards might affect my parents, who were expecting me home by tea-time. I'd been down to Winchester to see a friend who had just started a teacher training course at King Alfred's College. The fact that he had moved on, while I was still at home, re-taking my A-levels, may have created an itch of dissatisfaction in me. Why go straight back to all the familiar routine? Why not go to Bristol? Or Barnsley?

I discovered the answer to the second of these questions at 6 o'clock that evening, when I was dropped at dusk beneath sodium lights in a semi-urban wasteland where no further lifts were forthcoming. Turning southwards again already, I walked and walked until I succeeded in hitching a lift to Sheffield, and from there went to Chesterfield with a mussel-seller.

What were mussel-sellers doing, travelling from Sheffield to Chesterfield? Had I stumbled on to part of some traditional Great Mussel Route, which yet survived amid the expanding network of motorways?

Autumns were colder in those days, and the next lift, to Derby, had me freezing in the open back of a Land Rover. I have no memory of this beyond the words in the diary, any more than I have of the driver who had taken me all the way from Hampshire to South Yorkshire. A further lift took me to the M1 slip-road, where I joined other hitch-hikers, a soldier and a student. Etiquette required you to walk past the queue and take your place beyond the other hopefuls, but this didn't necessarily mean that you would wait a long time. (In 1971, for instance, on the A11 north of Epping, a woman with small children picked me up because she'd already passed five other hitch-hikers and the idea of giving a lift had grown in her mind until it reached fruition as she approached my rather forlorn figure.) The soldier went first, and then the student; soon afterwards it was my turn, and I had the good fortune to be offered- a lift in a sports car with a radio. I travelled in style to Leicester services, which we reached towards midnight.

Being on the road was getting exciting again: I savoured the sheer romance of a motorway service station at an hour when I was usually asleep. And in fact, I had moved into a world not just of long-distance lorry-drivers and night-shift workers, but of celebrities and showbiz. For there, in front of me as I sat drinking coffee – there, walking through the cafe as casually as if it had been the *Top of the Pops* studio – were Dave Dee, Dozy, Beaky, Mick and Tich! Dave Dee! - whose lubricious record 'Bend It!' was, that very week, at No.2 in the pop music charts! Oh, it was all meant to be – the lift to Barnsley, the freezing ride in the Land Rover.... I could return to college and tell this story to an audience of envious fellow-students: while they were lying unconscious, ready to drag themselves into Kingston again on another Monday morning, I'd been mixing with a top pop group at Leicester service station!

More romance was to follow. At half past midnight I thumbed a lift from a man on a motorcycle (a Norton Dominator, apparently, though I don't now even recall such a make) who was going to Woolwich. Why not go to Woolwich? Life was providing such wonderful experiences that night: who knew what it might offer if I went to Woolwich?

In retrospect, it is extraordinary that I survived the journey at all: I'm not convinced that I wore a crash-helmet; the M1 was foggy and bitterly cold, and the Dominator suffered from a faulty light which the driver had to change at Toddington. I buried my face in his jacket for protection, and was numb with cold and stoicism until we reached London. But as we hurtled down the Holloway Road at 50mph, and crossed London Bridge at 3 in the morning, I was fully alert once more. Oh God, this was living with a capital L! By Deptford we were doing 70, my boots scraping the ground as we screamed round corners. Or so my diary tells me.

At 3.30 am I was in Eltham, south-east London. How it compared with Barnsley at 6pm I can't recall, but I doubt if there was much to choose between them. I could have thought about going home, to south-west London, but the adrenalin was flowing too freely. Why not go right down to the coast? I managed to hitch three lifts, but I had to walk a long way as well. By dawn I was in a lorry so heavily loaded with cans that it had to change into first gear to climb even relatively moderate gradients: some offers of lifts are best refused.

Outside Battle, in Sussex, I was interrogated by police who had spotted me from their squad car. My answers must have satisfied them that I wasn't an absconding borstal trainee, for not long afterwards I was eating a late breakfast in Eastbourne, and then travelling along the coast road.

My diary doesn't record this, but I have a distinct memory of falling asleep in the car only to be unceremoniously turfed out of it into the rain, on the extreme eastern fringe of Brighton, and of having to walk miles into the town feeling aggrieved at such treatment. In the end I decided that I must have annoyed the driver by my lack of entertaining conversation, or perhaps by snoring.

From here on, the element of romance began to fade. There was a long walk in rain to reach the A23 north of Brighton, there were more lorries, and, because I'd been going now for over 24 hours, there was more snoozing. As a result of dozing off I missed a turning and ended up in a place called Waddon, near Croydon. Somehow I managed to get a lift in this suburban area, and made my way to Sutton where, still savouring my break from routine – and, no doubt, beginning to feel uneasy about my likely reception at home – I drifted into a cinema and sat through the Hitchcock film *Torn Curtain*.

My return to New Malden on the 213A bus, which had for so many years taken me to school, dispelled any remaining vestiges of Jack Kerouac-style fantasy, while my parents' recriminations and evident relief at my safe return touched my conscience.

The following day a friend of theirs, who was installing a central-heating system in our house, took it upon himself to rebuke me in no uncertain terms about how thoughtless I had been. I resented this, coming from someone who wasn't even a family member. It was on the tip of my tongue to retort that I had at least seen Dave Dee, Dozy, Beaky, Mick and Tich at Leicester service station; but something told me that he probably wouldn't have been impressed.

## Michael Rosen writer and broadcaster

I used to hitch to see my brother who was studying Geology at Oxford in the early 1960s. One time I was standing just beyond the roundabout at Headington, trying to hitch home when an old (even then) Morris Traveller stopped for me. For those who don't know, a Morris Traveller is a Morris Minor whose back has been turned into a van with a wooden frame. The driver was a man in his early sixties, I thought.

"Are you a student?" he asked. I said, no, it was my brother who was a student.

"What does he study?"

"Geology."

This seemed to bring the conversation to a standstill.

"Do you do this journey very often?" I asked.

"Why? Do you think I'm driving badly?"

"No, no," I said. "You're doing fine."

There was more pause.

"Do you work at the university?" I asked.

"Yes."

"What do you do?"

"I teach."

"What do you teach?"

"English."

I had a sense that he wasn't very keen on spilling all the beans at once.

"At what sort of level?"

"I'm a professor," he said.

I told him I was studying English. I said I liked *Anthony and Cleopatra* but wasn't too keen on *The Knight's Tale*.

"Don't you like Chaucer, then?" he said.

"Not very much," I said.

We dribbled on about not very much and he dropped me off in west London and when I got home, I asked my father, who was a university teacher who the bloke could have been.

"Was he leonine?" he asked.

"What does that mean?"

"Did he look like a lion?"

"Well, kind of, I suppose."

"Then it was probably Nevill Coghill," he said.

"Who's he?"

"Probably the best known critic of Chaucer," he said. "He translated the whole of *The Canterbury Tales* into modern English for the Penguin Classics."


# Terry Fletcher editor of *The Dalesman*

I did quite a bit of hitching in my impoverished youth and perhaps the most instructive in the highs and lows of it was a trip to the Woburn Festival in 1968, the day after I finished my O levels. I walked out of my house in Harrogate, stuck out a thumb and got a lift to the abbey gates within five minutes. The festival weekend was certainly an education for a well-brought-up lad from the leafy suburbs but the hardest lesson was getting home. After a six-hour single lift there it took almost forty-eight increasingly hungry hours to get back as umpteen thousand bedraggled fans all tried to hitch out of Bedfordshire!


# Ed Riordan dairy farmer
## 'Cheeking the Czechs'

I was hitching through Austria on my way to Turkey. I got picked up by a young couple who were teachers and were moving from Germany back home after getting married. Consequently I was squeezed into the back of a VW Beetle along with every bit of their belongings. It was very uncomfortable and I suppose, by way of apology, they offered to put me up at their new house. It was a bit out of the way but, as I was now wedged in the car coupled with the fact that they were nice people, I went with them.

We arrived at their farmhouse, built for them by their parents as a wedding gift. That night they had some friends over and we were drinking Most – a very strong home-made cider. After dark, the party really got going and then it was time for what seemed to be the local sport, getting in a couple of rowing boats, crossing the river and landing on Czechoslovakian soil without getting detected by the guards. You could see the guard-towers against the night sky. I reckon we made a lot of noise giggling and splashing about, but after fooling around for a while we got back into the boats and rowed back into Austria.

Soon after, someone brought out a couple of old pistols, great big Webleys and started loosing off shots towards the Czechs. This had the desired effect, it seems, of making the border guards fire flares into the air and return fire (into the air, I was assured). More shots were fired; it was interesting that you couldn't get the girls to stop firing, but when the ammo ran out and after some yelling from both sides we went back into the house to listen to rather melancholy songs accompanied by guitar.

For them the whole thing seemed absolutely normal, the equivalent of knocking off a policeman's helmet one drunken Friday night in England. To me it seemed, in retrospect, rather dangerous – but not then.

The next day they gave me a lift for a few miles and I continued on my way. I never saw them again.

## Gareth Rees writer, artist, musician
### Excerpts from 'Peach Paradise Lost'

England, bleak mid-winter and Sunday. Who'd want to get out of bed? Who'd want to venture forth on such a cold, damp and dismal day? But venture forth I did. And it was the day of my nineteenth birthday. Hitch Portsmouth to Newhaven.

The original Israel idea was based on hearsay, the word of my brother. The farms – or kibbutzim to give them the local name – were important ideologically. Israel was, in reality, in the mould of Western capitalism. But the Jewish people had been around a lot longer than all sorts of economic systems and, in the end, the principle of family and collective was felt to be more likely to secure survival than relying on the competitive tendency found in twentieth-century metropolitan culture.

The farm I eventually got work in, for example, was funded by the Jewish agency which channelled money from America.

The evidence of conflict was everywhere. Walking through the sandy earth, my feet constantly turned up empty cartridge cases or bullets. Sometimes I'd find rusted helmets. I didn't find hand-grenades but others did. From what battles came these relics? Was it the war of 1948? Skirmishes after that until the Suez war of 1956? The First World War may even have been responsible, when the British had driven the Turks from the region. Lawrence had been in the vicinity with his Arab army as well.

One day, the news broke that we were to embark on a two-day excursion. It felt like time off school as some of us were loaded into the back of the farm lorry. The rest of us – me included – had to hitch a lift to the first point of call – another collective farm.

On the first night we stayed in a simple hut. We were visited in the night by the guard patrol. The men were young, fit and sun-tanned as usual. They put down their submachine-guns and we fell to talking. Their English was amazing. Pure Cockney! The farm was East End Jewish.

Some farms were based around a country of origin like this one. Others reflected a religious point of view or lack of one, like ours, which was Communist and atheist.

We travelled right up to the Lebanese border where I was enthralled by the sight of Mount Hermon with its cap of snow. Although I placed a foot underneath the border fence so that it was on Lebanese soil, I felt inner anger at this man-made barrier to freedom. I was always close to barriers I wanted to cross but couldn't – Egypt, Jordan, Syria. Self-perceived gangsters appropriating to themselves patches of earth. I knew that security gained was security lost.

In a barren, mountainous, lonely place, we stopped to look at the remains of a synagogue, thousands of years old. I looked at the Star of David engraved into the stone and I was moved. I'm not sure what the emotion was but it was profound. Perhaps it was awe over the feat of Jewish survival. Perhaps it was the survival of the religious instinct despite its mauling by those who throughout the centuries have sought to cover up nefarious acts beneath a flag of sanctity.

A van driver picked me up and we travelled south to Lake Galilee. The Golan Heights with its Syrian gun emplacements glowered in the distance. But, as I walked by reeds lakeside, I felt peace. I resisted that part of me which wondered whether this might have something to do with Jesus. As a student of the gospel short stories, I had of course been powerfully drawn to his personality. But the story of the crucifixion was less magnetic. The resurrection made up for it but my rational, scientific education hampered my credulity quite a bit in those days.

With four others I hitched and visited the remains of Caperneum and I was amazed at the tiny streets and dwellings. It was as though people in those days were a quarter of the size today. We went on to visit Nazareth or Bethlehem – I can't remember which, for the probable reason that I wasn't impressed. I suppose it had to do with tourism and commerce. Galilee hadn't been spoiled in this way, at least not in my experience of the region. We met up with those co-workers who had been fortunate enough to ride in the farm lorry and stayed the night on the edge of a lake in an excellent youth hostel. The six of us from Britain shared a little dormitory and it put me in the mind of a boarding school.

We returned to the farm the next day and, as I was trying to sleep, a strange, ominous rumbling noise came from the desert. I didn't realise it at the time but it was the sound of an army on the move. During my evening stroll in the desert, I'd spotted a stationary army jeep containing two soldiers scanning the emptiness with binoculars. I greeted the soldiers and tried to find a form of words which didn't directly say, "What are you up to?" Anyway, the answer was that they were studying desert flowers.

When I awoke in the morning, I discovered that overnight the place had been transformed into an army base. Bulldozers had gorged holes in the desert to hide communications vehicles. Tel Aviv buses, their blue paint smeared with mud, were disgorging partially uniformed soldiers. Everybody seemed to know what he had to do. There were no screaming officers. On the trailer going out to the fields, steel-helmeted soldiers were already in trenches. Somebody drove towards us at high speed in a tractor. He screamed hysterically. There would be war by the afternoon. Eighty thousand Egyptian troops had flooded over into Sinai. The border was just five miles away.

As I set about my job of sorting out the irrigation pipes for peach saplings, I felt an air of unreality settling down over my activity. The threat of war seemed very real. It was time to leave Israel. It was time to leave now.

The word was that some countries were sending in planes to get their nationals out. Somebody suggested calling the British embassy to see what their response to the situation was. We went to the communications hut to use the telephone but, when we entered, we found the place occupied by high-ranking military. Radio transmitters were crackling and our friend Aron, the soldier-poet, seemingly the main man, was pointing things out to the assembly on a map. When he saw us, he screamed at us to get out.

I teamed up with Steve and Roger, two fellow British workers on the farm, to hitch a ride with a freight lorry to Tel Aviv. We traipsed the streets looking for travel agents. They were doing excellent business selling air tickets to rich people. They hardly had the time for us who were looking for something far cheaper. At last, though, we obtained some cheap tickets for Cyprus on a ship sailing from Haifa that night.

It was only a short journey to endure and the next morning we awoke to find ourselves anchored off the Cyprus port of Limassol. What to do? How to proceed? We decided to look around the island while we pondered these questions. We hitched a ride from an air force padre from one of the British bases. In the middle of a dry, brown panorama of countryside, we saw an emerald oblong. The air force had flown the turf from England! The padre took us to a beach reserved for British officers, their wives and children. After a spot of tea, the padre, who admitted to having time on his hands, drove out of his way and finally left us at a sleep little sea-side town called Paphos. As we explored these environs I suddenly noticed I was walking on a mosaic. Someone shouted and I realised a couple of people were doing their best to uncover some antiquities.

We headed inland and up into the Troodos mountains. A British air force Landrover, on its way to a surveillance post on top of the mountains, stopped for us and terrified us by leaving the road and driving crazily over rough ground. They left us at the summit of Mount Troodos where the cold was shocking.

At the summit was a café for tourists. We noticed an English couple and we took a table near them. Speaking loudly so that they would hear us, we discussed the plight of our situation. And it worked. The couple approached us saying how they couldn't have helped but overhear us. They had a hire car and were shortly going back to their hotel in the northern port of Kyrenia. They could fit us in their car. It was grand to get out of the cold.

The couple went to their hotel and we slept the night nearby on the beach. In the morning, the couple returned with a carrier bag of food for us. They said it was given to them by the hotel because of the hotel lunch they were missing whilst they day-tripped.

Even though a conflict was taking place in Cyprus itself, we felt safe to be away from Israel. I parted company with the Britishers I was travelling with – Steve had got a job in Nicosia and Roger secured passage on a ship to Greece before arriving back in England a few days later. I was on my own and free to continue my travelling.

# Julia Oseledko 25-year-old great traveller and true dreamer

Hitch-hiking is a way of life – a means of exploring the world. Through hitch-hiking you can even learn something about geography. For example, my knowledge of Serbian geography was very poor before I went there. Now I know that there are mountains and valleys, ski regions, places for rafting, reserves and even canyons.

Hitch-hiking allows the possibility of seeing the world as it is – different from that shown on TV. I recollect my trip to post-war Serbia. My friend and I found ourselves on the main street of Belgrade with huge bags and the desire to do some sightseeing. The railway station (and the luggage lockers) were far away; the tourist information point had already closed. So we walked along the high street among the souvenir shops and numerous stands selling maps and postcards. We stopped at one of them and asked for a map of Serbia and some postcards. The seller (whose name was Alex) gave us a few postcards of Belgrade for nothing, saying "Keep this as a souvenir of my beautiful city." He asked us where we were from. We found out that he was an ex-hitch-hiker, easy rider and simply a very kind man. We left our bags near his stand and went to enjoy this splendid and romantic city on the Danube.

We returned to Alex and he was kind enough to put us up for the night. We talked for a long time about city life during the war and the post-war situation. He told us how he sheltered a lot of people at his flat during the war and how NATO bombed the city centre. But the people were not angry – on the contrary they have become more helpful and hospitable; they have changed their views, ideals and priorities.

## Philip Tremlett  borough surveyor

In the early 1970s, three friends and I hitched a lift out of Plovdiv in the open back of a blue van on which was written in English, 'Made in the USSR'. It was a lovely ride in warm sunshine. At one point, as the air was flooded with the scent of lilac, I thought I was in paradise. We were passing through a valley whose sides were clad with blooming lilac.

Arriving in Sofia, the capital of Bulgaria, a policeman 'ordered' us to go to the state-controlled travel agency. Freelance tourism wasn't tolerated. But we didn't want the official agency. We knew they'd send us to a western-style hotel with western-style prices which would savage our remaining funds. Nevertheless, we made our way to the agency, passing several interesting sights on the way. There was a propaganda poster in the form of Mick Jagger under a hairdryer. We also passed a huge, modern tourist hotel and spied diners in an expensive restaurant setting. It seemed an incongruous sight in a supposedly egalitarian country. Outside the restaurant was a big crowd of people gawking at an American Ford Mustang sports car. I felt disdain, perhaps mixed with a bit of jealousy, for the rich tourists eating their rich meal. I thought, with some arrogance as well as conviction, that our more basic travelling was superior.

# Let's Improvise

# Pinch "short, fat underachiever now drumming for The Damned"

How did I miss my lift home, and how could I have let my only chance of a floor for the night wander off as I was aimlessly bumping off walls trying to cut through the fog of snakebite and black imbibed earlier that evening? These were painful questions to ponder as I settled down in the pub doorway, trying my best to shelter from the beautifully typical English summer rain. So I would sleep here until the early hours, then make my way to the on ramp of the A1 north and homewards to victory by way of thumb. Or so I thought.

As the early morning delivery trucks thundered their way past me, not twenty feet away, with their amphetamine-fuelled, hairy-arsed drivers in their warm cabs, I had the nagging thought at the back of my mind that I need not be here at all. That I hadn't spent all that money last night, that I did still have some cigarettes left, and this was just a bad dream.

A quick, almost defeatist, search of the pockets turned up nothing more than I had expected. A ticket stub to the beer-and-vomit-filled pus pit that had been host to the Destructors gig last night, and a beer mat with the phone number of some crusty old wench who had appeared as tempting as Marilyn Monroe through my (obviously defective) beer goggles.

Fortunately it got light early, and I made my weary way the two miles or so to the A1, casually waving a hopeful thumb at the rumbling juggernauts. It was early, and the traffic was light as I hit the side of the motorway with a renewed enthusiasm, fuelled by the unlikely reasoning that the bigger the road, the more likely the chance of a lift.

What I hadn't realized in my youthful ignorance was (I was sixteen, and not really too bright with the ways of the world), dressing in filthy ripped jeans, a studded leather jacket with The Exploited painted on the back, and sporting a slightly wilted eight-inch bright red Mohican, were not the best ways of attracting any kind of good Samaritan for my virgin foray into the world of hitching.

After the umpteenth truck had bellowed past, giving me the horrors with that unbearably loud air horn they used that seemed to scream: "NO FUCKIN' CHANCE MATE!!!!! ", I hit upon a really smart idea. I took off my stinking T-shirt (also bright red) and wrapped it around my head to divert attention from the dangerous hairstyle that was obviously stopping people from picking me up. Now I was looking like a tie-dyed Lawrence of Arabia after a particularly bad psychedelic sand storm, but was convinced it was the answer to getting me back to my minging squat in Grantham that at the moment was beginning to feel like the Hilton in comparison to this Hitching Hell.

I had now walked about four miles, and was approaching an on ramp from some non descript little village off to the left. A car was there, not accelerating onto the A1, but just idling temptingly for me to run up and be saved.

As I got within thirty feet of it, the door swung open and some old battleaxe screamed at me with her husband-battering voice: "You've got to be fuckin' kidding!" and sped off, no doubt thinking she'd got one up on the filthy punk youth of today. Now it wasn't too easy running on slippery, squidgy grass in 14-hole Doc Martens that had soles as smooth as a ballerina's slippers, and I managed a half-hearted "Fuck you!" to the fast-disappearing tail lights of the rusty blue Escort.

I had heard from friends about the hitcher-baiting game of stop, crawl, drive off, often accompanied by insults, and now it had happened to me. Fuck!

So I plodded on, back to the traffic, holding my thumb in the way Roman emperors used to when they were deciding on life or death for fallen gladiators and feeling total empathy with them in this arena of transport hell. After what seemed like forever, I came upon a petrol station with a pub/hotel attached to it, and slowly ambled past, checking the scene like some hungry eagle would scour the ground for a rabbit in the open. Up against the side wall of the pub was leant a bicycle. Unattended. Salvation!

I would grab my trusty steed and cycle the remaining 15 or so miles home, gaining much-needed exercise in the process.

I had just grabbed the handlebars as the cellar door flew open and some giant ginger-haired demon came flying at me, cursing and yelling at the top of his lungs about what he was going to do to me. Now the shock of this pot-bellied ginger giant merely being in my bubble was enough to send me scuttling off back to the side of the road, without all the threats of mutilation etc, and fortunately for me he gave up the chase, wheezing and hacking after about only fifty yards.

I was Daley fuckin' Thompson in comparison, and made the getaway with ease.

So, back to the old routine of thumb out, windows down, abuse, air horns and total and utter despair. I walked about another five miles, all the time fantasizing about my mattress on the floor and the unhygienic sleeping bag on top, wondering if I still had that half-eaten tin of beans in the fridge, or whether my squat mates had thought of me as they quaffed it the night before. Just then, a BMW slowed and pulled in to a lay-by shortly ahead. Another fuckin' comic, I thought, but the driver leaned out and shouted "You want a fuckin' lift or what?!"

I sprinted to the open passenger door and eased myself down into the cracked leather seats, surrounded by a haze of cigar smoke and the unmistakable whiff of unwashed armpits. In an almost inaudible gasp, I told my saviour (who looked not dissimilar to Boss Hogg off *The Dukes of Hazzard*) that I was going to Grantham, about twelve miles up the road.

After five minutes of meaningless small talk, and an over-glamorized version of my meeting with the ginger giant, he felt comfortable enough to start telling me of the 'unusual' sexual habits of him and his wife, of how they enjoyed an 'open' relationship and weren't averse to bringing different partners home for mutual enjoyment. Now call me naive, but I was genuinely interested, and encouraged the conversation for the next few minutes, wondering what kind of poor souls could be tempted back to the lair of Boss and Mrs Hogg (who probably looked like the female equivalent) for some nasty flesh party.

Then he came out with it: "I only live a few miles past here, in Bottesford, why don't you let the wife knock up some breakfast for you and give those rags of yours a wash?"

Hmm.

It clicked then that I was destined to be the filling in some sweaty Hogg sandwich, and the thought turned my stomach more than the now almost blinding stench of the unwashed business shirt that was hanging stiffly about his considerable bulk. I think I almost chirped like a budgie as I demanded he let me out at the upcoming Grantham turn-off. Not my nearest turn, I would still have to walk another three miles, but an early escape, which was definitely in order, judging by the glint in Hogg's eye. I almost fell out of the Beemer when he had slowed enough near the turn-off, and waved him on his way, mentally showering the near-miss of Hogg heaven out of my mind. Who in their right mind would want to do this hitching lark, I thought, as I headed the last weary few miles back into town.

I had got about halfway, and with the morning sun burning down, making the hangover sweep over me in waves, I just had a complete energy drain and decided to catch a few minutes' sleep on the fluffy grass verge. I had just drifted off when I was woken up with a shout of "What do you think you're doing, son?"

I looked up, startled, to see a beefy Grantham cop snarling at me with all the affection he would show to a piece of shit on his shiny black boots. After relating the hitching horror story, which was met with shoulder shrugs and sadistic little grins, I asked if he could give me a lift into town, seeing as he was going that way.

"No fuckin' chance," came the eloquent reply, "But if you can empty out your pockets, I just want to make sure you're not carrying anything illegal."

"I'm not carrying ANYTHING," I assured him, just as I reached into my jacket and felt something in the lining. I pulled out a crumpled packet of ten Embassy cigarettes that inside held a screwed-up five pound note.

More than enough for me to have caught the train from Stamford to Grantham.

Bollocks!

## Sir Ranulph Fiennes writer and expedition leader

When I was a teenager, my Scottish cousin and I decided to hitch-hike from Sussex to Paris. We considered this very ambitious. We managed to make it to Dover but in France found it impossible to catch any lifts. In a drivers' café we were told they only pick up females. During the summer holidays a year later we tried again, this time wearing kilts, and were rewarded with immediate success.

## "BG"/"JK" bricklayers
### 'Dress Sense at the Isle of Wight Festival'

We were apprentices – bricklayers – and we decided to go to the Isle of Wight Festival, the second one. Not because we were in the scene but, I think, we didn't really understand what it was going to be like. We'd just heard about it and decided to go. Well, we set off and, of course the thumbing was part of it. And I suppose we seemed… we looked a bit strange because we had our suits on because it was holidays, you know, and we had suitcases – none of your backpacks. Well, when people picked us up and we said where we were going, they looked at us as if we were mad. Anyway we got, I think, three lifts to the ferry – the last lift was from a bunch of hippies, going to the festival, in an old Army truck, and at first they thought themselves a bit superior but then Jimmy (my mate), started talking with them. He has a way, you know, even then he was a bit up front, especially with the birds. Well, they couldn't wait to get rid of us, and they had one bloke who must have been given the job of telling us to get lost. But he couldn't do it, he just kept saying (he had a really posh accent): "Look guys, we really like you, but..." He went on and on and we just let him. Eventually, we let him off the hook and made our own way there. Needless to say, when we got to the Festival some people thought we were in fact being very trendy – you know, like we'd done it on purpose, the suits and the cases – but we didn't really realise until later on. We were so covered in mud and so filthy (we didn't have a tent either) that we got the train back to London after it all. I never thumbed again but I picked a few up over the years, if they looked all right.

# Gabriel Morris for more information on the author, visit his website
**at gabrielmorris.bravehost.com**

A few summers ago, I was hitch-hiking with a couple of friends from Oregon to New Mexico. In the middle of the Nevada desert, we found ourselves in a bit of a rough spot. Perhaps foolishly, we'd decided to traverse Nevada and Utah via Highway 50, the 'Loneliest Highway in America.' From Fallon, about an hour east of Reno, we got a ride another twenty miles – to smack in the middle of nowhere.

There was only dry, desolate desert as far as we could see. A rusty, bent barbed-wire fence creaked eerily nearby – the only sign of human existence other than the scorching pavement. Only the most hardened vultures would've been happy to be there. We soon realized that we were probably the loneliest hitch-hikers in America.

The unrelenting sun beat down on us. After two hours, hardly a handful of cars had passed. Our desperation was soon mounting, along with the temperature rising on the backs of our sunburned necks. We built a small shade tent to escape the glare, using our backpacks and my friend Bethany's shawl.

Eventually, we started hitch-hiking in both directions. Any car that was going away from there was a car that we would crawl into. Finally, my friend Forest came up with a plan. He said that if we really wanted a ride out of this desert nightmare, we had to envision what we wanted – and then ask for it in clear and plain terms. Having little else in mind to help our predicament, we decided to give it a try. We huddled under our makeshift structure and figured out what, in our delirious state of despondency, would be the ideal ride. Namely, anyone friendly who was going a hell of a long ways and would be arriving shortly to deliver us from our otherwise certain doom. We then voiced our humble request to the empty desert – and to whatever benevolent forces overhead that may have noticed our pitiable condition, and waited.

Thirty minutes later and, just as we were beginning to wonder if the travelling gods had forsaken us, an old Subaru station wagon passed our trio of outstretched thumbs. We all groaned in sweaty dejection. Fifty yards down the road, however, the car turned around and came back, did a U-turn, and then stopped right in front of us. The driver got out.

"Hey, guys! You look like you could use a ride outta here. I was gonna keep going, because I didn't think there was enough room for the three of you and your bags in my little rig here. But hey, we'll put some stuff on top and see what we can do."

We were, of course, ecstatic. We showered him with adulation and guilt, to ensure that he'd make the room to bring us along.

Drew was a lively young college student, headed from California back to his home state of Colorado. He tied what he could on top of the car, and then we managed to squeeze ourselves in. Three days later, after perpetual driving, wind-blown hair and good music, and contemplative nights spent on the barren floor of the expansive desert, he dropped us off safe and sound in the heart of the Rocky Mountains. We arrived at our final destination later that night, weary but eternally grateful.

## Annie Nightingale DJ and broadcaster

My first holiday in the expensive South of France was as a pretty well penniless teenager, with three others: two boys and another girl. Having tasted the vulgar delights of the Croisette at Cannes late at night, we then had to find a way back to Mandelieu, where we were staying. Shamelessly, my friend Janice and I paraded along the seafront ostentatiously thumbing lifts. The two boys meanwhile hid in nearby shrubbery. As soon as a car driver stopped to offer us a lift, we hopped in, followed immediately by the boys. Not big, not clever, not particularly original, but it worked!

## Sarah March garden designer

Having booked a last-minute end of season cheap deal (yep cheap and nasty) to a place near Hania in Crete, my friend and I were looking forward to a week of sun, sand and ouzo. When on the first morning we realised the beach near our hovel consisted of grey boulders, we decided to catch a tour bus the following day to a beach called Elafonisi. The beach delivered – pure golden sand, an island to wade out to and sand dunes to claim as your own. After a day of bronzing ourselves (OK, more like over-cooking), we waded back across to the bus stop to realise the times on a leaflet we'd acquired were for the high season and the bus had left 30 minutes previously. There were a couple of tour buses left but they wouldn't let us on and the drivers simply pointed north!

OK, we thought, better start walking. After forty-five minutes on a heat-miraged road (tumbleweed wouldn't have looked out of place), we decided to stick out our thumbs, not expecting much luck as there was nothing ahead and only building sites or new developments behind. But we thought luck was on our side when a cement mixer groaned to a halt beside us. Thankfully we jumped in – and almost jumped out just as quickly. OK, after a day of sunning ourselves we probably didn't smell too sweet, and I guess after a day on a building site under the fierce sun it was inevitable – but Jesus, the whiff! Thanking God for small mercies, the driver, a middle-aged man, was at least wearing a vest, once white, and a pair of shorts, short being the operative word – but heck, we needed a lift.

We remembered most of the bus ride down to Elafonisi as being picturesque – the route went through a wonderful gorge, chestnut groves, postcard hillside villages and passed more than a couple of Billy goats gruff. We also remembered the bus driver showing due care and attention and hooting before turning blind corners. Not Mr. Cement Mixer! The scenery was beautiful but took on a different ambience through slitted eyes too petrified to open fully. This guy drove like a maniac – full speed on the straight and on the bends, didn't bother to toot on the hairpins and I'm sure he scraped the stone wall separating us from a deep ravine and certain death on more than one occasion. Then at a small village – not really a village more like five linear houses and a bar – he decided to stop and motioned towards the bar itself. Fantastic we thought – need some ouzo to calm our nerves – but when we started walking after him he frowned sternly at us, uttered something in Greek, which we could tell wasn't called for, and then we realised it was men only, as with most of the village bars in Crete. He stuck ten fingers up and so we thought OK for ten minutes we'll just sit in the shade; anywhere other than the cab where his distinct aroma lingered even when he didn't! After all, he had been kind enough to pick us up and he probably stopped here every evening.

After an hour of throwing stones at a mangy looking cat to keep it away from us, he came out far jollier than before and off we sped. As you can imagine, the units consumed did not improve his knowledge of the highway code and he now also stank of fish. He belched frequently and noisily and then, to our disgust, farted! The smell was almost coma-inducing. If my eyes had been open they would have been smarting from the noxious fumes, and for someone who breathes the majority of the time through her mouth, my nostrils had never been blown so quickly. I figured smelling it was worse than ingesting it. Strangely, though, despite having almost killed us on the road and subjected us to his burps, he was completely mortified at what he had done. He hastily opened all the air vents in the cab (even though the windows were open) and started to sweat even more than before. He kept muttering things which we could only assume were apologies, and didn't belch again for the rest of the journey. We were sure he even drove with his arms pinned to his sides to save us from his sour armpits.

Soon after we arrived at Maleme and he indicated we could catch a bus from here back to our fleapit. When we leaped down from the cab he looked truly sheepish (or should that be goatish!) and his eyes were downcast.

This was five years ago and we still haven't found out whether it is a mortal sin for a Cretan man to pass wind in front of a woman; perhaps he's still 'Hail Marying' somewhere...

## "LS"

### 'For a Few Kilometres More'

I always thought we were ground-breaking – people of my generation hitching. It didn't occur to me that it had been going on before. But I got a lift in sporty Ford Capri from this middle-aged chap who was obviously gay, well-spoken, dressed in these ridiculous, as he called them, "short-shorts" – kind of white tennis shorts, but short. Anyway, he picked me up and was pleasant enough and soon mentioned that when he'd been at Cambridge in the fifties, he used to hitch down to the South of France every summer. He said the best lifts were from "queers" and if it meant them driving you a good distance with "one hand on the steering wheel and one hand on your cock," then that was a small price to pay for the open road. All you needed to do was wear a pair of "short-shorts" (I must have sniggered at that point) and away you went.

By the time he'd finished his story, it was time for me to get out anyway – but he wasn't threatening at all and I wasn't worried. When I got into college, I told the story and sure enough three other guys said they had encountered this chap already – the "short-shorts."

So he was cruising, it seems, all that term, since he did pick me up again, but I made it clear how it was going to be and he said, "I'm not queer – not at all – you have to prostitute yourself from time to time, don't you ?" Well, at the time I maintained I never would, but later, stuck in some godforsaken bit of Italy, I admit I coaxed a few more kilometres out of one driver. There you are – all character building."

# Julia Oseledko 25-year-old great traveller and true dreamer

**'Extreme Nights'**

A tent plays a significant role in a hitch-hiker's life. It gives you the chance to feel independent. But there is drawback – every night you musk think about where to put it!

'The night problem' is a major concern. There are different ways of overcoming it: you can hitch-hike all night long – this works, but you should do it in pairs. You can sleep at train stations, you can use Hospitality Clubs or stay with friends or just put up a tent.

I'd like to give an example of an extreme night and an unusual place to camp. In Zhica, a small village in Serbia, at 7 pm, having missed the opportunity of getting accommodation in a monastery (which was closed), we asked the locals where we could put up a tent. They recommended the orchard in the monastery grounds. During the night we were bombed by falling apples and in the morning we looked out of the tent and saw… another tent and a motorbike! The monks were disconcerted but just continued to walk around and pray.

# Chris Lewis transport journalist

I joined the queue of hitch-hikers with my 'Birmingham' cardboard sign (it really was a case of joining a queue in those days), when a greasy chap sidled up to me and said: "There's a driver over there heading your way now," pointing to the truck park. A ten-minute search revealed no such person after which I returned to the slip road and there was no sign of my greasy friend – he'd struck lucky in my absence and his ruse to get my place had worked. Well, I was very young then...

Another long wait and a friendly chap, driving a knackered (Bedford?) eight-wheel tipper, steam gently rising from the wet cloth on the transmission tunnel – gave me a lift to the outskirts of Birmingham and then I walked down the Soho Road into town.

In Birmingham everyone told me, "Hitching? It's almost impossible!" (The motorway virtually starts in the city centre – there's just nowhere where drivers can pick you up), so I paid for a single on National Excess! I probably saved about 50p over a cheap student return.

# Snapshots of a Destination

# Sir Alan Parker film director/writer

I hitch-hiked across Europe after doing my A-levels in the summer of 1961. Well, 'Europe' is a bit of an exaggeration as we (my school pal Brian Stacey and I) only trekked through France to Spain, and then back again by way of Switzerland. The outgoing trip was remarkably easy, mostly because we cheated a lot with a train journey or two, when the going got rough and the rides dried up. The road back from Barcelona, I remember, was a good deal less romantic than Laurie Lee had led us to believe. An unscheduled long and rather hedonistic stay on the Costa Brava had left us perilously short of money, and we lived on bread and jam as we snaked along the Côte d'Azur on our way to Italy. Some days we couldn't believe the luck of the 'golden thumb' as car after car would stop and hundreds of miles would be covered. Other times, parched and hungry, a whole day could go by and it seemed that we'd travelled no further than the next roundabout.

Nights of star-filled skies, curled up in a sleeping bag beneath a canopy of (inedible) grapes in a dusty vineyard seem quite romantic now, but at the time it was misery as we parsimoniously allocated our remaining money for one proper meal every two days. I've never been so hungry before or since. We never made it to Italy because the lifts became scarcer the posher the place you were in.

For instance, no one in a Mercedes ever gave you a lift. I always thought it was strange that all those posh cars in Monte Carlo from Communist Czechoslovakia passed you by with their number-plates saying 'CH' – only to discover later that they were from Switzerland. In Monte Carlo we gave up the ghost on seeing a chalkboard sign outside a bus depot that said 'Geneva – 10 francs.' We promptly took the charabanc.

Hitching home across rural France was the leg I enjoyed the most. We even got a lift in a Mercedes, for over two hundred miles, from a bunch of rich American college kids who were driving the parental car back to England. I also have lovely memories of the sun on my face, snug in the back of a farm truck full of apples, and a more vivid one, stuck in the back seat of a 2CV with a giant randy, furry poodle that tried to bugger me but thankfully settled for my rucksack.

# Stewart Lee

### 'West From Walpi'

In the autumn of 2000, my partner and I were driving around the deserts of the American Southwest. It was a holiday, really, but I was also trying to research the area, and the culture of native peoples specifically, for a novel I was writing. It was hard to find out much about the Hopi, and all but impossible to read anything about their clowning tradition, which was what I really wanted to know about. I'd been a stand-up comedian for 12 years and I was sick of it. I had some kind of romantic notion that I needed to go back to the source. But due to a serious sense of humour failure by American government officials in the early 20th century, the Hopi clowns now clouded their performances in secrecy. Bizarrely, Henry Winkler, aka The Fonz, has a videotape of a Hopi clown gig, but he won't show it to anyone. The clowns recognised The Fonz as a fellow funny-man when he was seen in one of the villages, and allowed Winkler to film them as part of a sacred bond of trust. Not even the University of Arizona can match Fonzie's influence.

He is cool.

The Hopi occupy an increasingly encroached plateau, east of Flagstaff, north of Winslow, surrounded on most sides by the lands of the Navajo. The Navajo saw the writing on the wall a lot sooner than the Hopi. Monument Valley has been ceded back to them, and they control tourist access. There's no shortage of Navajo symbols on baseball caps and shoulder bags. They're probably the most media-friendly of the native American peoples, and, like good capitalists, have ultimately come to view the ongoing occupation of their country as a business opportunity. Good luck to them. The Hopi, however, have seen it all before. They survived Spanish invasion by ambitious conquistadors, and later fought off Navajo attacks from their fortress citadels of their high mesa villages. Hopi holy stories say they will inherit the earth. They have no reason to believe that the white man's presence, like that of all their other enemies, is anything but transitory.

And indeed, when you stand in the ancient cliff-top village of Walpi, surveying the vast empty desert from the roof of a low pueblo house, the rest of the world does seem very far away.

The Hopi's approach to tourists couldn't be more different to the Navajo's. There's only one place to stay in Hopi Land, and that's at the Hopi Cultural Centre. It's clean, efficient and has excellent blue corn tacos, but you feel you're there mainly to stop you getting in people's way and nosing about too much. In Walpi you ask at a little office and a somewhat reserved old woman will accompany you on a walk around the village. Walpi is the oldest continuously inhabited human settlement in the United States, not that the white officials in the tourist information centre at Holbrook, half an hour South, have ever even heard of it. The two Swedes who took the same tour as us asked the old lady questions about The Sacred Rock in the main plaza. The questions remained unanswered, and the Viking fools tampered with a clearly significant clump of feathers nestled in one of its fissures. I imagine that later on they were visited in dreams by vengeful Katsina spirits.

As we left Walpi, another old lady showed me some hand-carved sculptures of traditional Hopi figures. In Flagstaff and Tucson the souvenir shops were full of plasticised knock-offs, but here was a nine-inch wooden replica of a Hopi Mudhead clown carrying a rattle and an ear of golden corn, at a price I could afford.

My Mudhead figure was the closest I came to meeting a Hopi clown and I treasure it. Maybe if I'd stuck around, like the writer Frank Waters, who stayed in Hopi land the best part of a decade to write a story, I'd have made some inroads. But this was the strangest, most alien place I'd ever visited. And I felt that, just by being there, I was causing some indefinable offence.

So the next day we drove West away from Walpi. After a couple of miles we picked up a hitch-hiker. He was a young Hopi boy, in his late teens, wearing jeans and a work-shirt. It was midday, and he was walking maybe 20 kilometres from Walpi to see his girlfriend in one of the outlying Hopi settlements, I forget which one. He said there was some kind of ceremonial dance later in the week, but it was difficult to ascertain exactly what it entailed. After a while the three of us ran out of things to say. In the wordless gulf, *Electric Ladyland* was bubbling at low volume in the car CD player.

This is always what happens on the few occasions I've picked up hitch-hikers. Stifled conversation followed by a tense, embarrassing silence. But this was worse than usual.

In my mind, the Hopi were clown-mystics, utterly unrelated to my own culture, mysterious, far away and removed. What did I have to say to them, or they to me? As we let the young man out he said, "Hey, did you know Hendrix was half-Indian?"

"Yes," I said, "yes, yes he was, wasn't he?"

# Nigel West intelligence historian

My most memorable lift was in 1969 from a lay-by on the Moyenne Corniche just above Villefranche-sur-Mer, all the way to Florence. I was accompanied by a fellow English student from Grenoble University and we were attempting to reach Florence in time for Easter where we were to rendezvous with our respective girlfriends, one of whom was working at the famous Mach 2 nightclub behind the Piazza Santa Croce.

We had been promised free accommodation and plenty of other incentives to complete the journey.

After less than half an hour we were picked up by an Italian driving a left-hand drive saloon with Rome number plates, and he turned out to be the Cultural Attaché at the Italian Embassy in London who was driving his new car, recently purchased at the favourable diplomatic discount, all the way home. This proved to be a very comfortable ride, albeit an unexpectedly lengthy one, because he insisted on stopping at innumerable sites *en route* to improve our grasp of the history of the region. We stayed at a couple of hotels on the way, all paid for by our generous driver, and learned a great deal about many of the wonderful churches and remote hilltop villages that were within easy reach of the autostrada. The trip was made all the more enjoyable as our host kindly volunteered a further detour and drove his two grateful passengers right into the heart of Florence.

Ever since, I have been unable to drive past Villefranche without thinking of that hitch-hiking adventure.

# Vernon L. Smith Nobel Prize winner in Economics 2002; Professor of Economics and Law at George Mason University; President, International Foundation for Research in Experimental Economics

Maybe twenty-five years ago I flew in to Salt Lake City to give a lecture at the university. The cab driver drove out of the airport heading for town and right at the airport exit was a hitch-hiker.

The driver said, "Do you mind if I pick this guy up? I always like to help people who need a lift."

I said, "I don't mind at all. Let's pick him up."

So we did and I asked myself, "Where else besides Salt Lake City could this have happened?"

## Gareth Rees writer, artist, musician

Hitch-hiking across the Middle East to Istanbul, I passed through a town which looked as though it had been in a war, such was the destruction. My driver, an architect who spoke English, said there had been an earthquake a couple of days previously. He took me to his home where I had a bath, enjoyed a feast and was given a soft bed for the night.

If I'd arrived at Istanbul from the European west rather than the Asiatic east, its enchantment might have made more of an impact. For me, it meant the end rather than the beginning of the magic of Turkey. It was a giant city full of honking motor vehicles and hassle from vendors. It was Dickensian in the sense of unbridled capitalism. Everything was for sale. Everything was for purchase. Beginning to worry about my funds, I sold my saxophone in the Grand Bazaar. I missed it but not the burden of having to carry it.

## Billy Hayes General Secretary of the Communication Workers Union. He now travels by bus, trains, boats and planes. He keeps a weblog which is: www.billyhayes.co.uk

Kerouac's book *On the Road* wasn't well known on the Liverpool council estate where I grew up. His tale of hitch-hiking across the USA was famous amongst hitch-hikers. Highway 61, Route 66 – these names of roadways in the States sounded incredibly romantic. Travelling from town to town, not putting roots down, the freedom to wander – not knowing how to get there but hoping to find an adventure on the way.

The A580 didn't create the same feeling or seem anything like as exciting. To the kids of Croxteth it was, however, a big road to cross, one we were told never to go near and never to be there when the English Electric was "letting out." Because of this and our parents' obvious desire for our safety, it meant that we had to make sure we went up to the A580 regularly, just to see the speed of the traffic and to watch the 544 bus (a limited stopping service) racing along at what seemed like incredible speeds. The "lancs" was to us urchins our endless highway, at the end of which lay a place called Manchester, which was television land. If you were thinking of running away, that was the direction to go.

Croxteth is located in the north east of Liverpool and was part of the council planners' attempt in the 1950s to deal with the post war housing crisis. Together with the new town Kirkby, these were the overspill estates designed to turn the inner city of Liverpool into a rose garden with slabs of concrete and high rise flats to greet the 21st century.

Us overspill kids, we loved it – we had fields, a river, woods, cows, horses, a sandpit, and that road that led to other places, plus a gamekeeper called Percy.

At night from my bedroom window I could hear the roar of the traffic speeding along the "lancs", the lights in the distance were a magical display of strips of light, meaning travel. The first time I ever travelled that highway was when I was only 10 and my mate, Tony Lenniham, decided that he was going to leave home because he had been told off by his mum. He asked me to go with him and to me, this was too good an opportunity to miss, so I joined him. We made it as far as Haydock and because it started to pour down with rain, and having no money, we decided to go home and be better prepared next time.

Ten years later – 1973 – was my next time. Although I had done some hitch-hiking in the UK, this was my big chance.

By now I was once again ready to hit the road. Dave McGraw, my travelling partner, had read *Bound For Glory* by Woody Guthrie and was obsessed with similar tales of travel, so we decided that we had to see the world or some part of it before we hung up our desert boots.

Dave and I had met at evening classes; we had struck up a rapport through our mutual love of Bob Dylan and our dislike of the Religious 'O' level teacher. Dave had also been selected for a place at the London Academy of Dramatic Art and was hoping to become an actor. Me – didn't want to open boxes of salmon at John West Foods for the rest of my life. That seemed a good enough reason to hit the road.

After we had both saved our small fortune, we decided it was time to get going. I can still remember the big breakfast my mum cooked me the morning we set off, telling me to look after myself – I'm sure Woody's mum did the same thing.

Dave and I walked up to the East Lancs Road, stuck up our thumbs, bound for Europe. Looking back all these years later, it seems amazing that the use of our thumbs got us around Europe; perfect strangers driving lorries, vans, cars, would stop simply because you stood at the side of the road and waved your thumb and what's more they welcomed you into the vehicle for the next part of your journey.

It took us twenty minutes to get our first ride. Strangely enough this took us as far as Haydock which felt like a centrifugal force keeping me within the orbit of Liverpool. We eventually made the next part of the journey south when a minibus pulled up full of people from Salford who told us they were personal friends of Graham Nash, of The Hollies and Crosby, Stills & Nash. This impressed us greatly, particularly when they showed us other signed album covers by Joni Mitchell and Nash.

We arrived on the outskirts of London at the end of the M1 and felt stumped because getting around London appeared to be the most difficult part of the passage south.

The then A&R man for the recently formed Virgin Records stopped for us and we felt that we were developing a musical theme to our travels. He told us that he had recently been at a party with the Stones and the only music that Keith and Mick would tolerate was a new sound called reggae which our driver was playing on his eight-track. We found it hard to believe that such music, whilst very popular at the Top Rank in Liverpool, would ever take off with more mainstream listeners and rockers, like the Stones.

By early evening we were at Dover, the edge of the known world, getting on board the ferry to Holland. This filled us both with marvel at our achievements. Having only ever crossed the Mersey we were now on our way to Europe.

We eventually alighted in Holland and it suddenly occurred to us that people spoke a different language, but not to worry, Dave had come prepared. Pulling out his copy of Ken Welsh's *Hitch Hiker's Guide to Europe*, we stopped cars and asked": "Der verg nach Aachen" – which was supposed to mean "the road to Aachen". Whatever Dutch people must have been made of us, as we spoke German words in a Liverpool accent.

As night fell we had the stars for our ceiling and the roadside ditch for our bed. We were too tired to open up the special fluorescent tent (which accommodated two). The following morning our thumbs were back in service in Germany. Our travel seemed to be swift, we made Innsbruch quickly, competition for lifts increased lots – Germans, Italians and Americans – who all seemed to have written on their backpacks 'Don't blame me, I voted for McGovern.'

We eventually hit Verona in Italy. Verona was special to Dave, being the site of the play *Romeo and Juliet*. It was also to hold other memories as we had to walk some way before we got a ride and Dave vomited on the streets of Verona, a plague on only one stomach. It was a wonderful place with the Armani suits and lots of smartly dressed Italians and grown men with handbags.

Then we were off to Florence, a most beautiful place, Michelangelo's David was something to see along with the scooter bikes.

Then on to Milan on the back of a truck with a drunken lorry driver who seemed oblivious to traffic lights and oncoming cars. Milan was a big shock, a big city with lots of big city problems. A night sleeping in a doorway was enough to persuade us to get to Rome.

As we travelled south towards the City on the Seven Hills, it became increasingly clear to us that two men with beards, who looked like they needed a wash, were not the first preference for the single male-occupied car. We hit upon an arrangement with girls travelling together that we would split each couple up. So that in order to frighten off the more amorous male, a man and a woman together often got the better lift. The trick was the last-minute switch. I can still remember the look of amazement of one motorist when he discovered he had just picked up two men to travel with him to Rome. Dave shouted out – "He's got Dylan" as 'Stuck in Mobile' blared out of his radio. It was a Maserati as well. Our driver had a face that was tripping him, as my mum would say.

Rome was an amazing place. Whilst not a superstitious person, when visiting the Colisseum, I could have sworn that I could still hear the screams of the Christians being fed to the lions... a spooky place.

Late that afternoon, we experienced the dark side of the great outdoors life. We met two girls from London and were convinced that the romantic side of our adventure was about to kick in. We spent hours talking to them about how you had to watch what you did and how you had to protect yourself, as if we had crawled through the deepest darkest forest and wrestled mountain lions; we told them it was best to keep their money in the bottom of their sleeping bags. After some time they had to get off but said that maybe they would see us in the park late that night.

We did see them later that night, they woke us up at 4.00 in the morning telling us that they had coincidentally been staying nearby to us and someone had tried to rob them. We discovered that Dave's sleeping bag had been slashed at the bottom, but no money taken. It was all embarrassingly obvious to us what had happened. Dave and I had let our libido get the better of our common sense. With lots of "OKs" we got our bags together and walked into the dawn of a Rome morning.

We spent the rest of that day viewing the Sistene Chapel. "Didn't it hurt his neck when he was painting?" I remember thinking.

Rome to me was my first real experience of a major foreign city, I could have been on the moon – so different and special. We spent a couple of days in Rome seeing the sites, walking the streets and realising that zebra crossings on the roads meant absolutely nothing to the motorists of that city.

Because Dave had to return to the UK, after one month in Europe we had to make our way back north to Venice where Dave would catch a flight to England and the beginning of his acting career.

# Steven Pinker Johnstone Family Professor of Psychology at Harvard University

During the summers my friends and I would take the Canadian National Railroad out west and bicycle around the Rockies and Vancouver. Tens of thousands of kids did this, with the support of the Canadian government, which sponsored hostels and campgrounds. I was poorly equipped and trained, and often broke down, bonked, or found myself on an impassable dirt road. I probably covered as many miles in pickups and vans as I did on the bicycle. I remember one day the sun fell earlier than I had planned and I was in pitch blackness without a light in rural Alberta. As if out of a dream, a van materialized, with other young people *en route* to a campground in Jasper, and room in the back for my bike. I sat on the front seat while Van Morrison's 'Tupelo Honey' played on the 8-track. I could just make out the zigzag silhouette of the Rockies against the starry sky. When we arrived I pitched my pup tent and the next morning awoke to the most beautiful sight I had ever seen.

# Eric Stoll IT consultant

I've been taking quite a few of these 'city breaks' in the last few years. What I've been doing is revisiting all the cities in Europe that I hitched to during the sixties and seventies. Back then, I seem to have been rather unimpressed by most of them, probably because what I was looking for in city was not the architecture or the museums and all that stuff which interests me now, but rather whether or not there was some kind of 'scene' as we used to say – music, like-minded people and all that – -a bit of action! So I would arrive somewhere, make a swift judgement and either stay or go. Sometimes that judgement took about half an hour, sometimes a little longer. For example, I hitched to Oslo as part of my 'Scandinavian campaign.' I arrived having hitched up from Germany, through Denmark and Sweden. I'd had a good time in Stockholm and had stayed a few days. However, after wandering about Oslo for half an hour, I decided it was not for me, so I hitched back to Stockholm. It was too easy; I went to Barcelona from Paris – not much here, I thought, so hitched to Madrid – a little better – stayed the night. Then on to Lisbon – a bit dead, so back to Marseilles – really good, stayed a while. I went on like this for years; free travel, as and when I liked. The fact that I could just up and go by simply sticking out my thumb – it was incredible when you think back.

Then I hitched with someone who was a little more sensitive to the conventional 'cultural' aspects of the destination – so I mended my ways, hence the 'city breaks'.

# "AR"

**Adana, Southern Turkey**

My companion Jeff and I hitched a ride on the back of a lorry and it was wonderful. The sky was blue. The sun was hot but tempered by a breeze blowing in from the sea. The coast-line was magnificent with wonderful beaches: a tourist paradise but there were no tourists except for the odd individuals like ourselves. Landward was a biblical scene of peasants working in the fields and horses going round and round winnowing grain. Clouds of chaff blew into the sky. Quite often, incredibly almost, the remains of ancient cities would come into view. Peasants grazed goats on the grass between the columns of temples from which civilisation we didn't know. As we surveyed all of this, we ate the provisions we'd bought in Mersin, rubbery white goat's cheese, cucumber and bread.

When our lorry dropped us off, it was as though we'd been dropped off the twentieth century as well. We waited for hours in the heat of the day but no motor vehicle approached for us to beg a ride. The road wasn't tarmac. It was a road fashioned by the feet of humans and their flocks over centuries. After a while, we stopped fretting over the 'need' for progress. The Western clock just stopped ticking. It was timeless and nothing really seemed to matter. I looked at the six-foot-long, black, dead snake lying by the roadside. I didn't think, didn't interpret. The dead snake was a dead snake.

The sun began to lose its intensity and flocks and shepherds passed us by on their way home for the night. Some shepherds hailed us and indicated for us to go with them. Jeff and I looked at each other. Why not?

We headed inland into fertile, green, hilly country. After half an hour or so, we arrived at our destination, a hamlet of stone dwellings. We were led up to a flat roof where women in colourful dress were laying a bed of beautifully embroidered carpets and quilts. Overhanging the roof was a mulberry tree bearing ripe fruit. Sitting on the roof with the sun beginning to go down over the green valley, seemingly untouched by the twentieth century except by ourselves, engendered an enchantment that is hard to describe.

The women stayed apart and indoors along with cows and young goats and sheep. A girl peered at us, strange aliens that we were, from a doorway and then darted away when she saw me looking back at her. Perhaps she was called away by her mother to help with the banquet which was being prepared for us. We ate freshly made flat bread, haricot beans, yoghurt, honey, mulberries and peanuts.

There was a link with the twentieth century though. One of the men had left the village to get a city education. He was trying to learn English and to help him he had a battery-powered little record player and half a dozen records of English lessons. He had one other recording and it was by The Beatles. The 'B' side was one of my favourite songs, 'I'm Down.' Sulky words but the beat made me happy. I had to play it full volume though I felt sacrilegious imposing electric rock 'n' roll on that valley's ancient way of life. Our hosts, pointing to my guitar, wanted music from me and I played 'Jimmie Crack Corn.'

Night was on us suddenly. There was no electric light, of course, so our hosts left for their sleeping places and Jeff and I settled down under quilts on our flat roof and slept under the stars.

Next day, our friends who apparently did not work, came back to us and we rode on horses down to the deserted sand beach. Jeff stripped naked and jumped into the sea. I wondered if such nakedness accorded with local custom.

After a breakfast of flat bread, yoghurt and honey, Jeff and I decided it was time to rejoin twentieth-century haste. We took up position by the roadside once more. The dead black snake was still there. There was the same sense of stillness which seemed like an invisible barrier to the time-conscious world we were hoping to rejoin.

I saw agitation in the distance. Was this the twentieth century on its way to us? It looked like a dust devil. As it turned out, it was a truck. We offered, but the driver refused to take money from us. We assumed that in this part of the world, there was a code which commanded hospitality for aliens.

As the truck gathered speed, I was aware straightaway that we were on a collision course, a collision between twentieth-century haste and the ancient, slower rhythms of the country thereabouts. The road we were travelling had been fashioned by feet for feet and not for motorised vehicles. And the collision happened. We rounded a bend and before us, walking the road, were peasants and animals. There was a bump and I saw through the windscreen a man's body flying through the air.

The crumpled, bloodied body of an old man was carried onto the back of the truck along with his trilling, wailing, distraught wife. We left the man at a clinic in a small town. I didn't know if he was dead or alive. I did know I felt sick and wanted to be somewhere called home and I wanted mother-love. If the man had died, wasn't I, as a worshipper of the twentieth-century haste god, party to murder? It certainly wasn't an accident. The collision was inevitable.

# Bruce Northam his books include *Globetrotter Dogma: 100 Canons for Escaping the Rat Race & Exploring the World.* www.AmericanDetour.com

There will be moments when you don't know if you can visit a certain place. There will be a lifetime of knowing that you didn't. In 1922 my grandfather, James O'Sullivan, a captain in the fight for Ireland's independence, emigrated from Ireland to the United States via Canada one year after the partition of Ireland and simultaneously with the death of his associate Michael Collins. He travelled west, laying Canadian rails, cowboy-ranched in Montana, then hitch-hiked to Manhattan's Upper West Side, where he opened the popular O'Sullivan's Chophouse in a neighbourhood of Irish bars and ran it for thirty-five years. Shortly after establishing himself in New York, his wife-to-be also emigrated from Ireland. With this in mind, Mom and I visited Eire in tribute to her parents and to see if the Irish would reciprocate the hitch-hiking hospitality James O'Sullivan enjoyed in 1925 America. In this land of fiercely independent people who value their poets as highly as their warriors, our strategy was to be road-warrior day-trippers and elegant country inn evening guests – upscale vagabonds. At first, she waved at cars to request rides, but the drivers only waved back. We needed a hitching sign, so I crafted four cardboard appeals: 'Mom', 'Angel', 'Innocent', and 'Pub', which worked best at small town intersections. "So Mom, where should we venture today?" "Never ruin a hike with a reason," she winked. At that moment a car piloted by an eighty-five-year-old woman pulled over. We rode on narrow, stone-walled roads past thatched cottages, castles, fortresses, churches, and other noble dwellings. A prime-time radio talk show host mused about gardens and the comings and goings of birds in the yard. In the last fifty years it's been fashionable to sneer at tubris begonias. Magpie birdhouse raids scaring off other birds. The tits will come along quickly. Real world news. Then a lost pet alert followed by a stolen bicycle appeal. Mom reports, "Dad won't put out bird seed. He thinks it's welfare." The rain comes again. Our driver acknowledges, "The rain is fond of Ireland." The landscape changes to sheer cliffs, wet meadows, rocky moonscapes, and roofless abbeys. We pass a damp, lush, lime-coloured farm teeming with cattle. Pointing to cows, Mother chimes in with "onomootopoeia!" This enchanted Atlantic island foray reminded me of my mother's many traits – unconditional love, kindness, safety – and introduced me to others: she snores like a house on fire! We were in for a shock – we are dropped off at a pub, even though we were picked up using the 'Angel' sign. We ease into the social glue of pub life with a Guinness. Mom sits closer to the band playing music by the fireplace. Foot tapping gives way to knee slapping; soon she is dancing. Then it dawned on me – the sign I forgot to make for her, representing what my mom stands for: Love.

"Wherever they may in the distance roam, this country is never forgotten by its born." – Barman, looking over at my mother doing the Irish jig to live pub music

"Hugs remind us of who we are." – Mom

## Lars Therkildsen historian

After having spent half a year in Israel working in a kibbutz, a Dutch friend of mine, Rudy, and I decided in the spring of 1996 that it would be too ordinary to go home by airplane to our respective mother countries and decided to hitch-hike all the way back home instead. This was the beginning of one of the greatest adventures of my life. We started off in April, taking the daily mini-shuttle from the kibbutz to the nearby town of Ashkelon, where there was a road junction. Our mood was high, even though we were a bit nervous. Not so much for fear that something bad would happen to us, but more regarding how we were to find shelter at night until we got home. We didn't have a tent but had more or less just planned to improvise, whatever that meant – especially since I was almost completely broke. However, in the beginning we had a stroke of luck that made us forget all worries: In Israel it is in general very easy to hitch-hike, since it is one of the most common forms of transportation for the ever present soldiers. After we had been standing for only fifteen minutes at a dusty roadside at the Askhelon junction, a young couple pulled over and asked us where we were going. "Haifa!" we said. The coastal city of northern Israel was several hundred kilometres away, so we hoped they would take us some of the way at least. If they were going in the right direction. "It's your lucky day", the girl said. "We're going straight to Haifa." Rudy and I looked at each other: this was a good start. We had decided early on to take a boat from Haifa to Greece instead of the longer and potentially more dangerous trip through Syria and Turkey. That way we would also get some variation on the journey and a chance to see the pretty Aegean Sea. For a short while we considered finding work on a fishing boat going to Greece or Cyprus instead of paying the money for the three-day cruise, but the fear of being at the mercy of some mad fisherman on the open sea quickly made us change our minds and dig into our pockets. Thus the day after our arrival at Haifa we said goodbye to a beautiful but also troubled region, which had given us a lot of interesting experiences over the past months. I remember it as a very beautiful trip, but not exactly what I had seen in films, since we only bought the cheapest tickets and therefore had to sleep on the deck with a group of other backpackers. It soon got too cold for me during the night but luckily there was a cinema on the ship, where surprised guests would have their films disturbed every night by snoring sounds from somewhere in between the rows. After having reached Athens and played tourists for a few days, we soon got very anxious to get on the road again. We had already travelled many hundred kilometres and only hitch-hiked once. Where was the adventure? It was time to find a roadside and try our luck again. The plan was to go up all through the Greek peninsula until we reached Bulgaria. Soon after we had decided to embark on this whole trip, we had agreed on giving it an extra twist by hitch-hiking through Eastern Europe rather than going through the Western countries, which we more or less knew already. The Velvet Revolution wasn't long over and both of us wanted to experience what was left of Communist Eastern Europe before it was "McDonaldized" by Western business and life-style. For some reason however, none of the locals could agree on a highway out of the chaotic city. We ended up having to take a train to some smaller town, where we could finally pick up where we had left off in Haifa. From there began a long trip and some interesting days across the Greek landscape. This time we didn't have the same luck as in Askhelon. We had to wait several hours before someone finally stopped – a pattern that would haunt us the rest of the trip. Had we been two blonde girls, we would have had a lot more success. For just one guy, hitch-hiking is normally fairly easy, and for a guy and a girl too. But two guys is a combination that requires a lot of patience (not to mention two raincoats), since a lot of people worry about being robbed or worse, and are too afraid to stop. On the other hand, being two people – with at least one male – gives the hitch-hiker a feeling of security which is preferable on long trips. In general one should always use one's head and senses and be ready to turn down rides, if there is something dubious about the driver or the circumstances. Being two guys in good shape, however, me and Rudy didn't really bother about being too fussy – this would get us some interesting rides. Our problem was getting picked up in the first place! In the coming weeks we learned the importance of both being able to smile very warmly and at other times being able to look cold and desperate. We considered it dishonest to use the old trick of one of us hiding until a car stopped (to make it easier for the other one), and only did it once out of desperation. Instead, somewhere in northern Greece, where we had been waiting half a day, we came up with the idea of making a song-and-dance act out of The Supremes' 'Stop in The Name of Love.' It actually gave us some success. Most people, however, just thought we were dangerous lunatics and quickly drove by! When a long day of waving our thumbs at the side of the road came to an end, we found ourselves in the ancient town of Delphi. There we learned a key lesson in the art of long-distance hitch-hiking: bring a tent! After having had dinner we started to look for a hotel, but the small town was packed with tourist buses and every single hotel, hostel and boarding house was full. Our disappointment was beyond words – we were very, very tired. So what were we to do? We wandered the streets for a few hours, but with the absence of any Greek celestial miracles and with our eyes getting more and more heavy, both of us decided that any spot would have to do. We bitterly regretted not buying a little tent – no matter how tiny and cheap – before the trip. However, the night would not be as uncomfortable as we had feared: nearby we found a construction site, where the good people of Delphi had almost finished building yet another hotel, and after some initial hesitation we soon installed ourselves nicely in what I guess eventually would become one of the rooms. On top of it all, it seemed the construction workers were about to celebrate something the next day, because the room was filled with a lot of cardboard boxes with red wine, food and goodies. Maybe it was someone's birthday or maybe it was to celebrate that they had almost finished. After about thirty seconds of consulting with our consciences, the voice of our bellies was the only thing we could hear, and we finished all the food and most of the wine, eating and drinking as if we would never see food again. Even though we left well-rested and content in the morning, with our heads aching a bit, it was to be a sad celebration day for the construction workers of Delphi. From there on Rudy and I continued up through the Greek peninsula, where we experienced the beautiful landscape, and learned more and more of the art of hitch-hiking as well as the art of staying positive despite the long waits. With stops at Thermopylæ and Mount Olympus, the next resting place was in Thessaloniki in the north. The town was nice, but what I remember most clearly was that, when we were about to leave again and set about looking for a good place to be picked up, we passed a house where a very attractive Greek girl was having an argument with two men in the garden. Suddenly she saw us, said something very fast to one of the men, and rushed out towards us. She then pulled up her blouse and asked "Don't you think I have nice breasts?" Stuttering very badly, we could only agree. After having considered for a brief moment settling down for the rest of our lives in Thessaloniki, our journey continued.

# Brian Barritt

The road to Tindouf is an eight hundred and five kilometre plumb line hanging south from Bechar. It stops midway between the borders of Mali, Morocco, Spanish Morocco and Mauritania, over one thousand five hundred kilometres from Algiers. It's the end of the final line, the impasse of Algeria, after that the frontiers are defined by how much water you have and demarcated by the horizon. Only dry scrub and barbed wire grow in this kiln. The French planted the entanglements to stop their supply trucks being shot up by the Moroccans during their everlasting hostilities towards one another. They mined the border and fortified the tiny dry basin of Tindouf with a Foreign Legion fort of blazing red stone. Apart from lowering our profiles we have no logical reason to go there, it is such a ridiculous journey, but we figure something magical will happen so we start hitching the following day.

In Bechar we are invited to spend the night by a young Arab guy of about twenty-eight, dressed in a European suit and looking relatively 'respectable.' Thinking that it would be nice to kip in comfort for a night, we say yes and find we have accepted the hospitality of a police officer. Having informed us that he is a plainclothesman, and not without a bit of clout in the area, he gets out an automatic pistol and starts wagging it about. He wants to screw Liz is the idea, but we are so strange to him that he loses his way, and I am so enthusiastic about his automatic that he ends up showing it to me and letting me play with it. It's a snubnosed little bastard, about as ugly as they come, dangerous. During my army days I was posted to Cyprus; in the six months I was there more soldiers in the Royal Warwickshire Regiment died from accidents with guns than were killed by the Eoka terrorists. A one-second spasm of annoyance, or a lapse in attention, could blow this policeman away to Chief Headquarters in the sky. The trouble is he's not a rapist at heart, just a lonely guy gravitating towards the first bit of pussy to come through the area in God knows. I let him off with a suspended sentence, we don't have any trouble and I give him his gun back in the morning.

Our first lift from Bechar puts us off at the one-street town of Abadla and, while we are waiting for the next truck, we collect a crowd of ragged children around us. The kids are fascinated by the colour and texture of Davie's skin. They are only young, brought up since the French left and there's very few white kids passed through since then. They are running up and touching him, then pinching him to see if he's real, so we walk off down the road to escape them. But the crowd follows behind us growing larger and collecting some adults. Then they start throwing stones, so we are literally driven off into the desert and are lucky to get a lift that takes us a few kilometres, to a junction of the Erg Occidental on one side and the Erg Iguidi and the Erg Chech on the other.

(Ten years later, from the place where the kids threw stones at us and pinched Davie in amazement at the colour of his skin, the first French satellite was launched.)

Perhaps it was our garb that fazed them? Can't imagine why; I am wearing plain black drain-pipe strides that flare slightly at the bottoms – not those embarrassingly wide ones – these only flare a little and the flares are studded with small pieces of mirror which catch the light and bounce it about in crazy patterns. I only have to enter a coffee house to shower the occupants with globules of light and every time I move, haphazard designs flicker over the walls, ceiling and floor. Or Liz perhaps, wearing a green Kaftan in terrain that's not seen green since the Stone Age and bell-bottomed strides in bright multicoloured Paisley pattern that might, to Arab eyes, give the impression that the source of all nature resided at the top of them? Or Davie, dressed in scraps from the rainbow? And not a camel between us, stopping passing trucks by making magic signs with our thumbs – first of the psychedelic touaregs. For a few hours we sit by the fire of a brickmaker, chatting into the night in sign language and trying to find out what the huge hill in front of us is called, and whether the thin spire on top of it is man-made or a construction of the wind and weather.

The road to Tindouf is flat, like the desert each side of it, a dry rocky floor scattered with flints and pebble-sized fragments of stone. Far away things look bigger than they should in this flatland. That big bird is twice as far away as you think, hard rocky far away, barren bleached-yellow far away. Every so often rock buttes rear up out of the no-mans-land like orange-brown fortresses from some bygone age, their tops sculpted by the elements into spires and pinnacles.

These areas of gravel and small stones – regs – fill in the spaces between the ergs – sand seas – getting the land ready, as it were, to become undiluted sand. Antelope, elephants, ostriches all used to stalk about this land, along with lions and water buffalo; hunted and were hunted in a land that no longer exists yet is warm under our feet. Apart from horses, camels seem to be about the only things that didn't come from here, a couple of hundred years ago they were unknown in the Sahara.

These ships of the desert tread where man fears to tread, into the ergs themselves, with names such as Le Grand Erg Oriental. Names that to our fever-enriched minds conjure Califs, fantastic palaces and harems. The dusky limbs of the houris, discernible to the human eye in the exquisitely turned sand dunes, their breasts and bottoms quivering to the caress of the desert wind.

There is one single petrol pump in the entire eight hundred and five kilometres between Bechar and Tindouf, and if you're lucky one truck per day stops at it. Some time after midnight we get a lift atop a pile of planks and construction gear, along with half a dozen labourers imported to construct an artesian well at Tindouf. Exposed to an icy wind that hacks our faces with razor blades, we plough through the star-struck night. Davie has so many layers of clothing on him that he is the shape of a small barrel and his arms stick out from his sides like the wings of a penguin.

Every hundred kilometres or so we stop to make tea with water from a tank slung under the lorry. We run and gather armfuls of dried salt bush that seems to be everywhere, pile it in a heap and crouch round while it is set afire. The dried twigs go up like petrol, a single rush of flame that almost incinerates us in our boots and it's just about gone so we run and collect more, capering to keep warm while the water boils. The driver, holding a foot-long cone of sugar tucked under his arm, scrapes it liberally into the kettle. Dancing, giggling and pulling up armfuls of brush, then another blast of heat while we sit round blistering our lips on the tin mugs.

My right ear became infected on top of that freezing lorry; it started to hurt just before we arrived and my first impression of Tindouf is through a haze of pain. We arrive in the late afternoon. There is one part-built hotel and while we are at a café devouring camel stew someone goes to get the key from the schoolmaster. Tindouf is only now starting to get a few visitors for a couple of weeks in the summer, let alone the winter. Presumably because we are oddities and looking a bit wasted, we are given free use of a couple of concrete rooms, empty except for four old bed-frames.

# Billy Hayes General Secretary of the Communication Workers Union. He now travels by bus, trains, boats and planes. He keeps a weblog which is: www.billyhayes.co.uk

I had already hitched to Italy when I had the vague idea of catching up with a friend of mine who had gone to Greece, so would make the journey to Greece. Charlie Carter was meeting friends of his at Athens airport on 1st September and I had a week to get from Italy to Greece using my thumbs. Perhaps it is the self-confidence of youth that I thought it entirely possible to do this.

I was suddenly struck by the enormity of what I was attempting to do, all on my own. There I was in a foreign country, knapsack on my back, money in wallet, not speaking a word of the language and not exactly sure what the prospects of travel were in Tito's Yugoslavia. A Communist country, a non-Warsaw pact, but still Communist. After all those years of being warned by our teachers at school of the dangers of Communism, wasn't I taking too much of a risk?

I managed to catch a lift up to Trieste, the border town between Italy and Yugoslavia, and the Italian driver and myself simply smiled and nodded to each other. He indicated that he had a son like me with long hair and smiled some more; I gave him Wrigley's chewing gum, which Ken Welsh said in his book on hitch-hiking, was a good ice-breaker and a way of rewarding your driver – something of a bargain way to travel, if you think about it.

At Trieste it was clear that drivers were loath to take hitch-hikers across the border, lest the border guards discover drugs or, worse, bibles, and be put in prison for spreading degenerate Western values. This left me no option but to walk across the border, which is what I did.

Surprisingly, walking from the Capitalist West to the Communist East was a relatively simple experience; my passport wasn't even stamped. There I was in Commie land still breathing and not clapped in irons. No interrogation, no confessions to make, no lift.

If ever there was a country that hadn't caught the hitch-hiking craze, it was Yugoslavia. From about 8.00 in the morning I stood by the main slip road to the Yugoslav equivalent of a motorway. Cars with German, Italian, Greek, British number plates sped past, never stopping. Was one person by the side of the road more threatening than two? Did my beard and long hair really make me look too much like Charles Manson, the crazed hippie killer? Whatever the reason, it was clear that at my rate of non-movement I would never make Athens in time to hook up with my mate. It called for drastic action. Use some of your money, Billy, I thought. I decided to spend some money to get me out of this border bottle neck; I had to break the jam jar.

Boarding the Yugoslav equivalent of National Express felt odd; there I was a kid from the West, all the neatly trimmed hairstyles made me feel like an alien being. Nonetheless I had broken out. The next place would give me the chance to get my thumb out.

On to Zagreb. Now, there is a name for you, how foreign did you want to sound, a name that now reminds you of the wars of Milosevic but at the time, to me, meant foreign country, complete isolation.

After spending the night in a doorway of some tenement building – I felt that any building that looked too official would lead to me being arrested and my own version of *One Hundred Years of Solitude* in the Siberian Salt Mines. Another Billy Hayes at around the same time had been 'banged up' in a Turkish jail.

Travel to the edge of the city resulted in another day with thumbs up with zero effectiveness – not one lift, not one hitch-hiker either. I really was a stranger in a strange land.

Trains and boats and planes all cost money but as the delay began to eat into my travel time, another bus journey seemed to be the solution, so money had to be spent again. One more bus journey couldn't possibly break the bank, so bus journey it was.

The next day in the Yugoslav countryside seemed to be another day of lack of progress, until late in the evening an old jalopy of a vehicle trundled toward me and miraculously stopped. An old man and a young boy of about 15 offered me a lift, my luck was changing – a lift had met the challenge – I was motoring. Sitting in the cab of the vehicle was heaven, the boy even spoke English with an American accent; my Liverpool accent and his continued to clash until bit by bit we both slowed our speech down to very slow English.

"Sleep, sleep," he kept saying to me.

For some reason I couldn't bring myself to rest – yes I was tired but also tense and we seemed to be travelling away from where I was wanting to go.

"Sleep, sleep," the boy continued to say. As we approached midnight I came more and more nervous. What has this old man got planned for me?

"Sleep, sleep, Split, Split, Split," the boy kept saying as we entered the coastal town of Split. He had been telling me all the time that we were heading for Split and my nodding simply confirmed I was quite happy to go to Split.

When we eventually arrived in Split, the old man and the boy became animated about street signs and whether to go left or right, backwards or forwards, or perform a Balkan three-point turn. We eventually arrived at a police station where I was asked to get out of the vehicle and then invited to enter the 'cop shop'. In the police station I was greeted by the local police with wry amusement. At first I thought this meant the police of Split were going to put me up for the night. I was familiar with this, as watching Western television shows it was a common experience for hustlers with nowhere to stay to be offered a bed for the night by the local sheriff. I had heard tales of vagabonds in the UK smashing windows to get a bed for the night. The police did not indicate a cell in which to lay my head but asked me, in broken English, to empty my pockets and empty my bags. As all my worldly goods were splayed across the floor of the station, every item was sniffed – which was very brave of them in the case of my clothes. It then occurred to me that they were checking me for drugs. To the locals I obviously had the look of a drugs baron or a dealer, perhaps. Why someone who was dealing in drugs would choose to bum a lift along the Adriatic Coast had not occurred to them. Maybe they thought that all long-haired men smoked weed. Having spent the best part of an hour smiling at me, searching my clothes, they said "OK" and showed me the door.

By this time the man and boy had long gone. I was never quite sure if their lift to Split was a benevolent gesture or their attempt to crack down on hippies. On balance, it was probably the former, in which case they were probably as bemused as I was to be interrogated by the police and probably left to begin to prepare a letter instituting a campaign to free the 'Croxteth One.'

I walked out into the night, with nowhere to stay but my fluorescent tent – which was not much use if you were trying not to attract attention.

The next day it was back on the bus. No progress whatsoever on the hitch-hiking front. In fact I travelled the rest of the distance through Yugoslavia to Athens by bus and train.

After a day of wandering through Athens I decided that I needed somewhere to sleep for the night, so under a bush around the Acropolis seemed as good a place as any.

The next morning I made it to the airport. After a little while of wandering around I looked up and there sitting at a table were Charlie, Roz, Sheila, Doreen and Chris.

Thus, I made it all the way to Greece with (pretty much) just the use of my thumb, a little bit of subterfuge and a lot of ingenuity.

After Greece I travelled back through Macedonia and the Balkans all the way by car. I had good luck this time as just outside of Athens a green Volkswagen pulled up with three German girls heading for Aaken. They offered me a lift to Munich. I spent the next few months in Munich and Frankfurt before heading back to England, again using my thumb.

Those months spent hitch-hiking around Europe were amongst the most satisfying and enjoyable times of my early adult life. In many ways I wish I could have in some way paid the people who had helped me see so much of Europe for so little.

# INDEX OF CONTRIBUTORS

# LINKS AND FURTHER READING

Here is a short and by no means all-embracing list of websites, books, films and music which make reference to hitch-hiking.

## Some websites

**www.digihitch.com**

Peerless cyber-guide to all aspects of hitching, including articles, forums, advice, bulletin boards, pictures and countless other things.

**www.hike.ru**

Hitch-hiking news portal of the CIS region with a focus on hitch-hiking as a sport ('autostop'). Information available in Russian and English.

**www.suite101.com**

Magazine-style site featuring a hitch-hiking column with a moderate and loyal readership. It remains at Suite 101 as a dormant topic, and is also archived at: http://bernd.wechner.info/Hitchhiking/Suite101/

**www.livinghistoryfarm.org**

Website set up to "share the innovations of US agriculture and life in the past." Excellent section on the early history of hitching.

## Some fiction

*The Grapes of Wrath*, John Steinbeck (1939)
Depression-era 'Okie' migrants hit the road to California to escape drought and economic ruin.

*On the Road*, Jack Kerouac (1955)
This perennially hip, stream-of-consciousness travelogue is perhaps the finest literary exploration of hitch-hiking, even if its protagonist, Sal Paradise, only does it for part of the novel. Every archetype of patron and passenger appears.

*Fear and Loathing in Las Vegas*, Hunter S. Thompson (1971)
Brief sequence where a hitch-hiker is frightened out of a lift he has been given by drug-addled journalist Raoul Duke and his attorney.

*The Hitch-Hiker's Guide to the Galaxy*, Douglas Adams (1979)
The benchmark sci-fi comedy novel in which Ford Prefect, a reporter for the eponymous book, saves his friend from Armageddon by hitching a lift with a spaceship.

## Some guidebooks some may be out of print

*The Hitchhiker's Field Manual*, Paul DiMaggio (1973)

*Africa for the Hitchhiker*, Fin Biering-Sorensen and Torben Jorgensen (1974)

*Europe: A Manual for Hitch-Hikers*, Simon Calder (1985)

*Hitchhiking in America: Using the Golden Thumb*, Dale Carpenter (1992)

*The Seagoing Hitchhiker's Handbook: Roaming the Earth on Other People's Yachts*, Greg Becker (1994)

# Some films

*The Hitchhiker* (1933, director: Arvid E. Gillstrom) 'Two-reeler' comedy.

*It Happened One Night* (1934, Frank Capra) Clark Gable and Claudette Colbert go on the run (or thumb) and discuss hitch-hiking methodology.

*Hitch Hike Lady* (1935, Aubrey Scotto)

*Hitchhike to Heaven* (1936, Frank R. Strayer) Minimal information available on this, perhaps a prequel to *Hitchhike to Hell*?

*Hitchhike to Hell* (1937, Pat Carlyle) Cautionary moral tale about an innocent young girl who drifts into prostitution, murder and, er, hitch-hiking.

*The Grapes of Wrath* (1940, John Ford) Salutary adaptation of the Steinbeck classic.

*Sullivan's Travels* (1941, Preston Sturges) Black and white comedy about a showbiz type (Joel McCrea) who slums it as a hitching hobo, meeting Veronica Lake on the way.

*Hitch-Hike to Happiness* (1945, Joseph Santley) Romping Hollywood musical.

*The Hitch-Hikers* (1947, Connie Rasinski) Short animation.

*The Hitch-Hiker* (1953, Ida Lupino) The first in a filial line of scare movies about psychotic hitchers who insinuate their wicked ways into the lives of ordinary decent driving folk.

*Les Petits Matins/Hitch-Hike* (1962, Jacqueline Audry) Tale of independent woman who hitches her way to the Côte D'Azur by exploiting various male motorists.

*HWY: An American Pastoral* (1969, Paul Ferrara) Hagiography of rock deity Jim Morrison. He attempts to wave down cars with his jacket, finally gets a lift but then the original driver disappears...

*Hitch-Hiking* (1972, Frank Vitale)

*Hitch-Hike* (TV Movie 1974, Gordon Hessler)

*Autostop Rosso Sangue/Death Drive* (UK title)/*The Naked Prey* (US title) (1977, Pasquale Festa Campanile) Stylish Italian thriller about a journalist (Franco Nero) and his wife who pick up a shady hitcher while traversing the USA.

*Hitch Hike To Hell* (1977, John Buckley) B-movie oddity which reverses the conventions by presenting a motorist who rapes and murders any hitch-hiker foolish enough to step into his car.

*The Hitch-Hiker's Guide to the Galaxy* (1981, writer: Douglas Adams) TV mini-series sprouting from the radio show and books.

*The Hitch-Hiker* (US TV series 1983-1991, various directors) A hitch-hiker introduces various stories with a fantasy/sci-fi element.

*Andrea's Story: A Hitchhiking Tragedy* (TV Movie 1983, Robert Mandel) Sensationalist silliness.

*The Hitcher* (1986, Robert Harman) Serial-killing hitch-hiker (Rutger Hauer) gives the noble pursuit a bad name.

*The Hitchhikers* (1989, Alan Bergmann)

*Avtostop/Hitch-hiking* (1990, Nikita Mikhalkov) Soviet-Italian-Swiss-made comedy.

*Hitchhiking Vietnam* (TV Movie 1997, Karen Muller)

*Fear and Loathing in Las Vegas* (1998, Terry Gilliam) Screen version of the Gonzo epic, with petrified hitch-hiker (Tobey Maguire) sequence intact.

*Stopar/The Hitchhiker* (2000, Karel Janak)

*Hitchhiker* (2003, Danny Bourque) Short about a hitcher and his patron arguing about their respective philosophies of life.

*The Hitch-Hiker's Guide to the Galaxy* (TBA, Garth Jennings) After years of difficulties in developing the classic for the big screen, it is now (at the time of writing) in post-production and due out in 2005.

# Some music

'Hobo's Lullaby' – Woody Guthrie (1944) & Arlo Guthrie (1972)

(The legendary folksinger Woody Guthrie travelled across the USA by thumb, rail and foot and was reportedly inspired to write 'This Land is Your Land' while hitch-hiking to New York City in 1940.)

'Hitch Hike' – Marvin Gaye (1963)

'Cloudy' – Simon and Garfunkel (1966)

'America' – Simon and Garfunkel (1968)

'Hitchin' a Ride' – Vanity Fair (1970)

'Hitchhikin' Woman' – Warren Zevon (1970)

'Sweet Hitchhiker' – Creedence Clearwater Revival (1971)

'Walk on the Wild Side' – Lou Reed (1972)

'Black Throated Wind' – Grateful Dead (1976)

'Hitch Hiker's Hero' – Atlanta Rhythm Section (1976)

'The Hitch-Hiker' – The Doors (1978) (poetry and music released posthumously)

'On the Road' – Cold Chisel (1980)

*The Pros and Cons of Hitch Hiking* – album by Roger Waters (1984) (features a naked female hitch-hiker on the front cover).

'Bound for Glory' – Neil Young (1985)

'Comin' Home' – Eric Clapton (1988)

'Deathwish' – L7 (1991)

'Highway' – David Francey (1992)

'I'm Hungry' – Sugarcubes (1992)

'Hopin' For A Ride' – The Meices (1993)

'If He Tries Anything' – Ani DiFranco (1994)

'Hitchin' a Ride' – Green Day (1997)

'Tribute' – Tenacious D (2002)

# THUMBS DOWN: SOME AMUSING REJECTIONS

Hitch-hiking has passed me by. **Michael Grade, Chairman of the BBC**

Interesting. I have some stories, but from 50-60 years ago, and though I like the idea, am so utterly inundated with demands I just can't think about it. Sorry. **Noam Chomsky**

I am afraid I have never hitched a lift in my life – except from my wife when she is going to Waitrose. Sorry I can't help. Hitching and hiking are not for me. I walked down to the bottle bank once. Quite enough exercise. **Ian Anderson, singer/flautist with Jethro Tull**

Sounds like a great idea but I don't think I have any good anecdotes. (Unless you count being a fan of The Hitch-Hiker's Guide to the Galaxy as a geeky teenager.) Thanks for asking though and good luck. **Jon Spencer**

As I have never hitch-hiked in my life nor, rather meanly, have ever given any hitch-hiker a lift, I'm afraid I cannot supply a contribution for your book. Sorry. **Alan Ayckbourn**

It never occurred to me to travel at all, let alone travel in this way. Later, when I could afford a car and went on the road as an entertainer, there wasn't any space in the car to offer anyone a lift! I lived in the car and every bit of space was filled with clothes, props and the dross of life.
**Paul Daniels, entertainer**

Sorry but it is so long ago I cannot help. **Tony Benn**

Believe it or not, I have never hitch-hiked – I have always preferred walking.
**James Lovelock**

I am terribly sorry but I have never hitch-hiked, and as most of my life has been spent away at sea, I have never given many people a hitch, nor were there any funny stories. Like the idea though. **RKJ (Robin Knox-Johnston)**

Although I have hitch-hiked and carried hitch-hikers, no anecdotes have ensued. Thanks for asking, and good luck with the book. **James Gleick**